The Seed Within

Bible Study

Leah Vintila

WestBow
PRESS®
A DIVISION OF THOMAS NELSON
& ZONDERVAN

WestBow Press books may be ordered through booksellers or by contacting:

WestBow Press
A Division of Thomas Nelson & Zondervan
1663 Liberty Drive
Bloomington, IN 47403
www.westbowpress.com
1 (866) 928-1240

Unless otherwise noted, all scriptures are quoted from the NIV version of the Bible

ISBN: 978-1-4908-9572-7 (sc)
ISBN: 978-1-4908-9573-4 (e)

Print information available on the last page.

WestBow Press rev. date: 12/14/2016

This book is dedicated to our daughter, Emily, the greatest unexpected blessing of our lives, and to the honor and glory of our Precious Lord and Savior, who knit her together in her mother's womb exclusively for us.

The Seed Within Table of Contents

<u>Bible Study Destination:</u> This study takes individuals on a scriptural journey to experience a life fulfilled in partnership with God...a journey that ends with a final destination of abundant fruitfulness and a spiritual harvest.

Foundation Scripture:

> *"Blessed is the man who trusts in the Lord, whose confidence is in Him. He will be like a tree planted by the water that sends out its roots by the stream. It does not fear when heat comes; its leaves are always green. It has no worries in a year of drought and never fails to bear fruit." (Jeremiah 17:7–8)*

Focus of Chapter: The soil refers to the internal status of each of us and includes that which affects the heart and soul. This chapter focuses on purifying our hearts and minds as the first substance necessary for abundant growth.

Foundation Scripture:

> *"Those who sow in tears will reap with songs of joy. He who goes out weeping, carrying seed to sow, will return with songs of joy, carrying sheaves with him." (Psalm 126:6)*

Focus of Chapter: The chapter looks at the seeds planted in our lives that will ultimately grow within our hearts for either fruitfulness or fruitlessness.

Foundation Scripture:

> *"I (God) will send down showers in season; there will be showers of blessing." (Ezekiel 34:26)*

Focus of Chapter: This chapter focuses on how the Living Water of the Holy Spirit effectively enhances our spiritual growth and why alterations are sometimes necessary to further propel that growth.

Foundation Scripture:

> "I will lead the blind by ways they have not known, along unfamiliar paths I will guide them; I will turn the darkness into light before them and make the rough places smooth. These are the things I will do; I will not forsake them". (Isaiah 42:16)

Focus of Chapter: This chapter encourages learning from the wisdom that only God can give and using spiritual gifts to effectively enhance spiritual growth in ourselves and others.

Foundation Scripture:

> "The field is the world, and the good seed stands for the sons of the kingdom. The weeds are the sons of the evil one, and the enemy who sows them is the devil." (Matthew 13:38)

Focus of Chapter: This chapter focuses on the external things that the enemy uses to stunt our growth; These are the things that affect the mind and can have devastating effects on Christians if not removed.

Foundation Scriptures:

> "But the fruit of the Spirit is love, joy, peace, patience, kindness, goodness, faithfulness, gentleness and self-control." (Galatians 5:22–23)

> "The one who sows to please the Spirit, from the Spirit will reap eternal life. Let us not become weary in doing good, for at the proper time we will reap a harvest if we do not give up." (Galatians 6:8–9)

Focus of Chapter: The series of chapters concludes with a study of our ultimate destination to live a life in the abundance and fullness of Christ where fruit of the spirit is overflowing to the point that others are affected.

Chapter One: Fertile Soil

Outline

I. Conditions that Establish and Promote Fertile Soil
   A. Salvation
   B. Positional Sanctification
   C. Relationship
II. Components of Fertile Soil
   A. Faith
   B. Hope
   C. Trust
III. Components of Non-Fertile Soil
   A. Fear
   B. Idolatry
   C. Living in the Past

Foundation Scripture:

Blessed is the man who trusts in the Lord, whose confidence is in Him. He will be like a tree planted by the water that sends out its roots by the stream. It does not fear when heat comes; its leaves are always green. It has no worries in a year of drought and never fails to bear fruit." (Jeremiah 17:7-8)

Introduction:

Fertile soil refers to the soil conditions necessary to promote growth - a spiritual growth that can lead to abundant fruitfulness. Remember, all seeds must have soil in order to grow. If this was not the case, apples would spout trees on our kitchen counters, would they not? Of course they don't because the seeds need the right conditions. In the same way, an apple tree planted in the ground may grow, but it would be virtually impossible for it to bear fruit without the proper soil conditions that would provide for its fruitfulness. Your goal in life is not to just be a tree, but to be a fruitful tree; a tree that bears much fruit in the likeness of the seed that was planted. In the same way that the apple tree needs fertile soil to produce fruit, the same is true for us. We must have fertile soil in order to experience the abundant fruitfulness that God has in store for us as Christians. So this is what our focus will be for this first chapter of study.

During this chapter of study, we will focus on:

- Definitions of natural and spiritual soil
- The necessary conditions that establish and promote fertile soil
- The components of fertile soil (faith, hope, trust)
- The components of non-fertile soil (fear, idolatry, living in the past)

Definitions:

Natural Soil – *noun*

1. A particular kind of earth: *sandy soil.*
2. The ground as producing vegetation or as cultivated for its crops: *fertile soil.*
3. A country, land, or region: *an act committed on American soil.*
4. The ground or earth: *tilling the soil.*
5. Any place or condition providing the opportunity for growth or development: *Some believe that poverty provides the soil for crime.*

Spiritual Soil - *noun*

1. A particular state of being
2. Your belief system, values, morals, and emotions
3. The place in which spiritual seeds dwell; The heart
4. The foundation for growth through the Holy Spirit
5. Any internal place or condition providing the opportunity for growth or development

In comparing soil to the human ability to individually and effectively grow healthy fruit, the soil comprises the condition in which we live spiritually. And not just spiritually, specifically within our heart and soul. In this beginning part of our study, we will focus on the internal spiritual conditions necessary to promote the growth we need to effectively travel the journey of our life's predestined purpose. Our ultimate goal will be to reach the specific God-chosen destination for our lives...lives that are filled with contentment in all circumstances...lives that bears fruit abundantly to produce a harvest ...lives defined exclusively by Christ for His honor and glory.

To help us understand the significance of soil, we should know that the term was first used in the Bible in Genesis 2:7 when God formed Adam from "*Adamah*". "*Adamah*" is used in the Old Testament to signify the ground or soil as something that brings forth life. God brought Adam to life through "*Adamah*" and "*Adamah*" was the source of fruitfulness given back to Adam through the relationship that he had with God. Today, it remains the most vital component of the fruitful life that we seek as Christians. Without it, it would be impossible to be abundantly fruitful, let alone create even one single fruit of the Spirit.

Special Note: In the Old Testament, *"Adamah"* is used to describe Noah as a husbandman in Genesis 9:20. A husbandman is one who cultivates something to be fruitful. The term husbandman is also used in the New Testament where Christ speaks of the Father as the "Husbandman," Himself as the Vine, and His disciples as the branches, the object being to bear much fruit, specifically fruit of the Spirit. (*John 15:1 KJV*)

Scripture Study: Sifting through the Word:

Read the Parable of the Sower in Matthew 13:3-9 and 18-23.

According to verse 19, what is represented by the soil in which the seed was sown?

_____

According to verse 23, what does the seed falling on good soil represent?

_____

How much fruitfulness is produced when a seed is sown in good soil?

_____

A key element of how this is possible lies within the verse itself. The Greek word for "understanding" in this verse is *Syneimi*, which means to bring or set together; to unite. The root of this word comes from two words (*Syn* and *Heimi*) which mean to send with or accompany. It is only possible for us to understand scripture because it is accompanied by the Holy Spirit as is confirmed in John 14:26.

<u>Conditions that Establish and Promote Fertile Soil</u>

- Salvation

According to John 11:25-26, what is the source of life? _____

According to 1 Corinthians 3:11, who is the only Foundation? _____

Read John 15:1-8. What is required to bear much fruit? _____

The Greek word for remain (KJV) or abide (NIV) is *"Meno"* and references place, time, and condition. In reference to place, it means "to sojourn, never depart, to be held and kept in continual presence." In reference to time, it means "to continue to be, to last and endure, never to perish, and to survive all things." In reference to state or condition, it means "to remain as one."

Re-read John 15:1-8 and apply a meaning from each of the above to the blanks below.

Place: _____ in me, as I also _____ in you.

Time: _____ in me, as I also _____ in you.

State: _____ in me, as I also _____ in you.

Now apply those terms in your head to the following verse:

"If you (remain/abide) in me and I in you, you will bear much fruit."

- Positional Sanctification

Sanctification is defined as being set apart and made holy or righteous. The Greek word for sanctification is *"hagiazō"* which means "to render or acknowledge, to separate from profane things and dedicate to God, and to purify internally by the removal of the guilt of sin and by the renewing of the soul."

Special Note: The root word for the Greek *"hagiazō"* is *"hagios"* which means to be most holy or a saint. Interestingly, this root word also has two root words *"hagnos"* which means pure and *"thalpō"* which means "to keep warm and to cherish with tender love and care." Yes, deep within every part of our salvation, we find God's love and that is significant in consideration of our relationship with Him.

There are actually three different categories of sanctification: Positional Sanctification which occurs at the moment of salvation, Lifestyle Sanctification which occurs during our Christian growth as we strive to be more Christ-like, and Ultimate Sanctification which we cannot achieve until we are in the presence of God. For this chapter, we will focus on only Positional Sanctification as it is a qualifier for growth. Lifestyle Sanctification, while also important, will be discussed in more detail in chapter 6.

Positional sanctification refers to being separated apart, purified from sin and made holy at the moment of salvation. This is how impurities are removed from our soil to make us fertile as Christians. It is an instantaneous process that results in our imputed or implied righteousness as a result of Christ's death on the cross of our sins. The King James Version of Romans 6:5 tell us that *if we have been planted together in the likeness of his death, we shall be also in the likeness of his resurrection.* The words "planted together" in the original Greek text was the single word *symphytos* which means born together with, congenital, implanted by birth or nature, grown together/ united with. This word comes from two root words, *syn* and *phyō*. Syn (which you may recall from earlier in this chapter as a root word for "understanding") denotes a union and *"phyō"* means to puff or blow and is used in the bible to signify birth or springing up.

What other verse do you recall in the bible involving blowing to life?

I love knowing that just as God breathed life into Adam, He also breathed life into me at the point of my re-birth as a new creation. And as a new creation under the definition above, I know that I died to my sin through Christ's death...and was raised as one born together with Christ, implanted with His Holiness at my rebirth, and united with Him forever. Because this process is one in which we are grown together as one, it is impossible for me to ever be separated from Christ. And it's impossible for you, too. No matter how much you sin, you still have His DNA. No matter how much you are disobedient, you are still His. No matter how many times you fail Him, He still sees you with nothing but complete love because you are part of Him and have his imparted Holiness as part of you. There is nothing in the world you could ever do to change this fact. Absolutely nothing.

So if we are a new being, we have a new identity. We once were defined by sin, but now we are defined by a new life in Christ. The problem is, many of us still live as if the old definition applies to us. We haven't yet made the transition in our minds that the Holy Spirit already made in our hearts when He took up residence there and physically, emotionally, and spiritually redefined us...separating us permanently from our old selves. To effectively experience abundant growth, we must come to a full understanding in our hearts that we are defined by Christ and marked by Him, rather than by the world or our past or anything else that might want to take up residence in our soil. Remember, God doesn't see us through the same eyes that we see ourselves, He sees us only as He defined us through the blood of His Son.

According to Ephesians 1:4, why did God chose us in Christ before the creation of the world?

- Relationship

Who we are in Christ is a vital component of our soil if our expectant hearts are to receive the level of overwhelmingly abundant fruitfulness that we desire. Much to the dismay of God, many have made a public profession of faith and have a strong head knowledge of Jesus Christ, but have failed to truly know Him on a heart level. He pursues us relentlessly, yet many fail to recognize and yield to the immeasurable adoration and love He has for us.

According to the following scriptures, what relationship do we have with God?

John 1:12 _____

Galatians 4:6-7 _____

Romans 8:16 _____

Ephesians 5:1 _____

Why does Ephesians 5:2 say Christ gave himself up for us as a fragrant offering and sacrifice to God?

_____

According to John 3:16, how much does God love us?

_____

Why do we love, according to 1 John 4:19? _____

According to Romans 8:38-39, what can separate us from the love of God?

_____

In John 15:9-17, Jesus makes a powerful statement about the love He has for us and how we should love Him and others in order to experience complete joy.

What does this passage also say we are to Christ if we love like He commands?

☐ *We are His acquaintances*　　☐ *We are His friends*　　☐ *We are His followers*

The same scripture continues to state that we did not choose Him, but He chose us.

For what reason did Jesus say He chose us? _____

Yes, God love is amazing enough that He could see a greater purpose in us and specifically chose us to be His fruit-bearers. Jesus explains in John 15:8 that it is to His Father's glory that we bear much fruit because it shows us to be His disciples. Not a little fruit. Not occasional fruit. But instead much fruit. Abundant fruit. Fruit that will last. That is what pleases God.

But it takes more than His love flowing through us to create the type of soil needed to generate that level of abundance to overflow. He desires to be our first love. When our focus remains on Him, the love He is pouring out on us combines with our individual faith, hope, and trust, and creates incredible fertility. As a result, we experience a tremendous outpouring of His fruits that will please Him and bring Him glory. This is possible not because of our own action in having faith, hope, and trust, but instead of what God gives back to us as a result of these components. For these components are the foundation upon which our testimonies are built.

Components of Fertile Soil

- Fertile soil is rich in **faith**

Read Hebrews 11:1. How is faith defined?

_____

Read the following verses that describe what will happen to those who have faith in the Lord. Write down what will happen to you if you have faith in Him.

2 Chronicles 20:20 _____

Psalm 31:23 _____

Psalm 37:28 _____

Psalm 97:10 _____

Proverbs 2:8 _____

Proverbs 28:20 _____

Matthew 21:20-22 _____

Romans 4:13 _____

Romans 5:1 _____

Romans 5:2 _____

Galatians 3:9 _____

Galatians 3:14 _____

Ephesians 3:16 - 18 _____

Ephesians 6:16 _____

2 Thessalonians 1:11 _____

James 5:1 5 _____

I Peter 1:5 _____

According to Matthew 17:20 how much faith do you need have to move mountains?

_____

- Fertile soil is rich in **hope**

_____

Special Note: The biblical definition of "hope" is confident expectation

_____

Read the following verses that describe what will happen to those who hope in the Lord. Write down what will happen to you if you have hope in Him.

Lamentations 3:25 _____

Romans 8:25 _____

Hebrews 6:19 _____

Hebrews 7:19 _____

Isaiah 40:31 _____

Read Romans 12:12. What specific instruction does it provide?

_____

Read Proverbs 23:18. What certainty does this verse provide?

_____

Read Hebrews 10:19-23. What does verse 23 tell us about how we should hold on and why?

_____

In this verse, the NIV uses the word "unswervingly" and the KJV uses "fast" to describe how we should hold on. The Greek word for this verb is *Katecho* and means to hold back from going away, to restrain or hinder, to take possession of. This has a deep meaning for us as Christians. It shows that enemy's lure on us is so strong that we need to be restrained and hold firm to Christ who took possession of us. Holding unswervingly relates back again to keeping our focus entirely on Christ. The enemy stands to our left and right at all times trying to distract us off the path that God has chosen for our life. Think of this as you would if your car were to swerve off the road and envision how devastating it can be when you find yourself no longer on solid ground. Remaining on solid ground is important for us as we seek spiritual growth. This correlates with what many verses, particularly those in the Psalms, refer to as a steadfast heart. When we persevere forward with our hands securely on the steering wheel and our sights directly in front of us, we are maintaining a steadfast position that will be much harder for the enemy to deter us from. As Psalms 84:5 says, "Blessed are those whose strength is in God, whose hearts are set on Pilgrimage." The word "pilgrimage" here actually is translated in modern English as "highway" with a root word that means "to lift up or exalt" or "to take the high way". Isn't that a great thought as we journey towards our ultimate destination of abundant fruitfulness? As Christians, we have someplace to go. Let's stay our course on the HIGH way to make sure we reach our final destination to His glory!

- *Fertile soil is rich in **trust***

  Carefully and thoughtfully read the foundation scripture for this chapter. What does it say to you?

  _____

  How early does trust in the Lord begin according to Psalm 22:9?

  _____

  Read the following scriptures and write down what each verse tells you will happen to those who trust in the Lord?

  Psalm 22:4 _____

  Psalm 22:5 _____

  Psalm 28:7 _____

  Psalm 32:10 _____

  Psalm 33:21 _____

Psalm 37:3-4 _____

Psalm 40:4 _____

Psalm 125:1 _____

Proverbs 3:4-6 _____

Proverbs 28:25 _____

Isaiah 28:16 _____

Jeremiah 17:7-8 _____

Daniel 6:23 _____

Nahum 1:7 _____

Romans 10:11 _____

Roman 15:13 _____

Read Psalm 9:10. Why does this verse say we should trust God?

_____

Isaiah 26:4 also describes why we should trust in the Lord. How is God described in this verse? Why do you think He is described this way?

_____

_____

Read Psalm 127. What point does this verse make and what promise does it offer?

_____

How does Psalm 119:9 say you can keep your soil pure?

_____

Components of Non-Fertile Soil

We use the word Non-Fertile to describe soil that is not pure because it inhibits fertility in the sense of spiritual growth and fruitfulness. We could also use the word impure or contaminated to describe this soil as it is truly contaminated with unwanted traits, behaviors, or sins that limit our ability to have an abundantly fruitful life.

There are three basic components that can take over our soil and make it lose its ability to produce abundant growth and the enemy knows how to use these well in each of our lives. His greatest attacks will always come against those things which alter the condition of our heart.

The question we should all ask ourselves is what consumes our minds? For whatever occupies our minds to a great degree controls us. And that which generally controls us has strong roots in our hearts. Is your mind filled with fear? Is it filled with things you idolize? Is it possibly filled with recurrent thoughts about your past?

As you ponder this question, don't simply focus on negative thoughts. Even things such as Christian activities can contribute to non-fertile soil if not directed by God for His purposes and His glory. For that reason, we should examine our motives in all that we think or do. Motives that are not pure also will create conditions that will not foster growth.

- Non-fertile soil is laden with **fear.**

  Fear is a natural reaction to many things in life and the enemy uses it very well to his advantage to stifle our growth. Components of fear can range from actual fears of disaster to fears of what others think. Insecurities are one of the most common devices of fear Satan uses in his schemes against us and God. He knows that if we are insecure, our focus is most often turned inward, making us in a great sense self-centered which always replaces Christ-centeredness. Are insecurities or fears holding you back? Write down some of them below:

  _____

  _____

  _____

- Non-fertile soil is laden with **idolatry.**

  The word idolatry may conjure up images of ba'al or asherah poles from the ancient days of the Bible, but Satan uses this unhealthy component much craftier today. Idolatry today comes in the form of money, people, and activity, including busyness. We can even be an idol to ourselves through our pride and discontentment. If any of these things apply to you, list them below.

  _____

  _____

  _____

- Non-fertile soil is laden with **the past.**

  Guilt, shame, and regret are three powerful negative emotions that can keep us bound to our past for many years. Are you experiencing these or any other chains from your past that you are unable to let go? If so, note them below.

  _____

  _____

  _____

- Non-fertile soil is that which is laden with **anything negative that defines a person**.

  Do you have any negative emotions or embedded traits that fit this description? If so, describe them below._

  _____

  _____

  _____

*R*eflection:

Where are you at right now in your life? How fertile is your soil?

Use the following chart to mark the level of fertility vs. non-fertility on a 0-10 scale (where 0=none and 10=as much as possible) for each of the following components.

10	10	10	10	10	10
9	9	9	9	9	9
8	8	8	8	8	8
7	7	7	7	7	7
6	6	6	6	6	6
5	5	5	5	5	5
4	4	4	4	4	4
3	3	3	3	3	3
2	2	2	2	2	2
1	1	1	1	1	1
0	0	0	0	0	0
FAITH	HOPE	TRUST	FEAR	IDOLATRY	PAST

Now insert your number of corresponding of soil components into the soil below using the first letter of each component. Use a red pen or marker for the positive attributes and a black pen for the negatives.

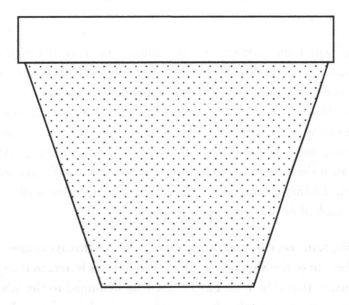

Are there any other components that make your soil fertile or infertile? If so, add them above now.

After you have completed creating your soil mixture, take a moment to reflect how this possibly has affected your life. Were you surprised to see how your soil turned out?

What should you ask the Lord to help you remove from your soil, if anything? In contrast, what should you ask the Lord to help you add more of?

_____

_____

_____

Be encouraged in knowing that whatever negative components we have in our soil, there is a scripture that provides a direct answer to how we can effectively make the transition away from it. We don't have to try to change our soil on our own, but instead simply have to rely on God to lead us to and through the necessary changes though Christ. Below is one such example.

If you currently have fear in your soil, what do Psalm 56:3 and Psalm 112:7 tell you that you should do when you are fearful or afraid?

_____

Relatable Bible Figure

For each chapter of this study, we will look at someone from the Bible in whom we can relate to the topic we are studying. For this chapter, Paul emerges as one from whom we can learn the most about this portion of our journey together.

Paul was born into a Jewish family and raised to be zealous with his faith. Originally named Saul, he carried the family tradition well and became one of the strongest Pharisees of that time, advancing Judaism more than many of his peers. When Christ appeared and later ascended leaving his apostles to form the church, Paul personally took it upon himself to attempt to destroy the movement through violent persecution of those trying to spread the gospel. He was zealously determined stop the Christian movement and planned a trip to Damascus to further fight against this cause. It was on the road to Damascus that his life would be forever changed. It was on that road that God would strike Saul down with blindness and dramatically redirect his path. Here is what we learn about that conversion from the book of Acts, beginning in chapter 4, verse 9:

> 9 Meanwhile, Saul was still breathing out murderous threats against the Lord's disciples. He went to the high priest 2 and asked him for letters to the synagogues in Damascus, so that if he found any there who belonged to the Way, whether men or women, he might take them as prisoners to Jerusalem. 3 As he neared Damascus on his journey, suddenly a light from heaven flashed around him. 4 He fell to the ground and heard a voice say to him, "Saul, Saul, why do you persecute me?"
>
> 5 "Who are you, Lord?" Saul asked.
>
> "I am Jesus, whom you are persecuting," he replied. 6 "Now get up and go into the city, and you will be told what you must do."
>
> 7 The men traveling with Saul stood there speechless; they heard the sound but did not see anyone. 8 Saul got up from the ground, but when he opened his eyes he could see nothing. So they led him by the hand into Damascus. 9 For three days he was blind, and did not eat or drink anything.
>
> 10 In Damascus there was a disciple named Ananias. The Lord called to him in a vision, "Ananias!"
>
> "Yes, Lord," he answered.
>
> 11 The Lord told him, "Go to the house of Judas on Straight Street and ask for a man from Tarsus named Saul, for he is praying. 12 In a vision he has seen a man named Ananias come and place his hands on him to restore his sight."

¹³ "Lord," Ananias answered, "I have heard many reports about this man and all the harm he has done to your holy people in Jerusalem. ¹⁴ And he has come here with authority from the chief priests to arrest all who call on your name."

¹⁵ But the Lord said to Ananias, "Go! This man is my chosen instrument to proclaim my name to the Gentiles and their kings and to the people of Israel. ¹⁶ I will show him how much he must suffer for my name."

¹⁷ Then Ananias went to the house and entered it. Placing his hands on Saul, he said, "Brother Saul, the Lord—Jesus, who appeared to you on the road as you were coming here—has sent me so that you may see again and be filled with the Holy Spirit." ¹⁸ Immediately, something like scales fell from Saul's eyes, and he could see again. He got up and was baptized, ¹⁹ and after taking some food, he regained his strength.

Saul spent several days with the disciples in Damascus. ²⁰ At once he began to preach in the synagogues that Jesus is the Son of God. ²¹ All those who heard him were astonished and asked, "Isn't he the man who raised havoc in Jerusalem among those who call on this name? And hasn't he come here to take them as prisoners to the chief priests?" ²² Yet Saul grew more and more powerful and baffled the Jews living in Damascus by proving that Jesus is the Messiah.

Although we don't know the exact time that he changed his name, we do know that after his conversion, Saul changed his name to Paul and went on to be zealously devoted to Christ. He influenced early Christianity greater than anyone else of his time with the growth of the church to the Gentiles. Why did he change his name? Some scholars believe it was because the name Paul was much more familiar to the Gentiles and they would more readily accept his gospel message as compared to the Jewish name Saul. Others attribute this to the meaning of the name Paul which means "little or small". Scripture tells us that Paul considered himself the least of men, a humble reflection that we should all model.

So how does this relate to this chapter of study? Some of us might have had a drastic conversion to Christianity while others were raised in the church and gradually grew in Christ. But we know that we all have a former self and all of us live in temptation of the world. Based on Paul's history of such violence against Christ, we know that he could have lived with strong self-condemnation against his past once he was unblinded to his behavior. Yet Paul remained fertile before the Lord, recognizing that his old self was gone and he was on a journey forward. We, too, can be like Paul by learning from his instructions.

What does Paul urge us to do in Ephesians 4:1?

Paul continues in Ephesians 4 to discuss impurities including some of those negative things we discussed that could be part of non-fertile soil. What does he say we should do to assure these impurities are not present in verses 22-24?

_____

_____

Aside from the negatives of our past that tend to corrupt our soil or those involving idolatry like deceitful desires, we recognized fear as a strong contaminant earlier in this study. Like us, Paul had fear, too, which could have threatened his fruitfulness.

Evidence of Paul's fear is found in 1 Corinthians 2:1-4. Of what was Paul fearful? Why is that significant?

_____

_____

God used this fear in Paul to grow his reliance on Him as God and to allow him to humbly recognize that He can do nothing by himself. This would be a powerful in assuring that Paul's soil was never contaminated by pride.

What did Paul ask for in order to help with his fear in Ephesians 6:19-20?

_____

Why does Paul tell us we no longer have to fear in Romans 8:14-15?

_____

Like Paul, we often face many things from our past and present that seek to contaminate our soil. Also like Paul, we have a future that was purposefully planned by the God of the universe. Never doubt the plans that He has for your life.

𝒟igging 𝒟eeper

Let it truly sink in that you are sanctified and God has incredibly great plans for you as part of your new life in Christ!

Read the following scripture from Jeremiah 29:11 with emphasis on the italicized word; Pause with each to focus on what the scripture is saying to you in the different context. Do you notice a distinct difference in the verse and the promise in each version? Write the difference in the space provided. The first one is done for you.

"For *I* know the plans *I* have for you," declares the Lord, "plans to prosper you and not to harm you, plans to give you hope and a future."

GOD has plans for my life. No one else anywhere at any time has the master set of plans, but God.

"For I **know** the plans I have for you," declares the Lord, "plans to prosper you and not to harm you, plans to give you hope and a future."

_____

_____

"For I know **the** plans I have for you," declares the Lord, "plans to prosper you and not to harm you, plans to give you hope and a future."

_____

_____

"For I know the **plans** I have for you," declares the Lord, "*plans* to prosper you and not to harm you, **plans** to give you hope and a future."

_____

_____

"For I know the plans I **have** for you," declares the Lord, "plans to prosper you and not to harm you, plans to give you hope and a future."

_____

_____

"For I know the plans I have **for** you," declares the Lord, "plans to prosper you and not to harm you, plans to give you hope and a future."

_____

_____

"For I know the plans I have for **you**," declares the Lord, "plans to prosper *you* and not to harm you, plans to give you hope and a future."

_____

_____

"For I know the plans I have for you," ***declares*** the Lord, "plans to prosper you and not to harm you, plans to give you hope and a future."

_____

_____

"For I know the plans I have for you," declares ***the Lord***, "plans to prosper you and not to harm you, plans to give you hope and a future."

_____

_____

"For I know the plans I have for you," declares the Lord, "plans to ***prosper*** you and not to harm you, plans to give you hope and a future."

_____

_____

"For I know the plans I have for you," declares the Lord, "plans to prosper you ***and*** not to harm you, plans to give you hope ***and*** a future."

_____

_____

"For I know the plans I have for you," declares the Lord, "plans to prosper you and ***not*** to harm you, plans to give you hope and a future."

_____

_____

"For I know the plans I have for you," declares the Lord, "plans to prosper you and not ***to harm*** you, plans to give you hope and a future."

_____

_____

"For I know the plans I have for you," declares the Lord, "plans to prosper you and not to harm you, plans to ***give*** you hope and a future."

_____

_____

"For I know the plans I have for you," declares the Lord, "plans to prosper you and not to harm you, plans to give you *hope* and a future."

_____

_____

"For I know the plans I have for you," declares the Lord, "plans to prosper you and not to harm you, plans to give you hope and a *future*."

_____

_____

ℬlessed 𝒜ssurances

- You were chosen by God to have a fruitful life; You were set apart by Him for plans that involve your fruitfulness.

- God abides with you in all places, at all times and in all conditions. He presence is continual; He will never leave you.

- By living according to the Word, your soil can be purified.

- God has made provisions for your life that allow you to have soil that is abundant in faith, hope, and trust...fertile soil that is capable of abundant growth.

- If you remain in Christ and He in you, you *will* bear much fruit.

ℱertilize 𝒴ourself:

> *"How can a man keep His way pure? By living according to your Word. I seek you will all of my heart; do not let me stray from your commands. I have hidden your word in my heart that I might not sin against you."- Psalm 19:9-11*

One of the greatest assaults the enemy has on us as Christians is the lure to believe lies against our identity. If he can have us forget the security of our identity in Christ, then we will cease to be fruitful which is exactly where he would have us. But the Word is very clear on how we can use scripture to overcome the evil one. The best defense against this is submerging ourselves in the truth to keep the lies the enemy casts at us from embedding in our soil. The first step is recognizing when our identity is not in Christ by paying attention to our thoughts and stressors. The second step is then turn our thoughts and attention to Christ by meditating on key verses of scripture or even listening to song that is filled with spiritual truths as a way of embedding the truth into our soil (heart and soul).

Think about the season you are in and identify one or more scriptures and/or songs that you can use to cover any lies with the truth. Then use those songs and verses often to assure that your soil is exactly as God created it.

Chapter Two: The Seed Within

Foundation Scripture:

> *Those who sow in tears will reap with songs of joy. He who goes out weeping, carrying seed to sow, will return with songs of joy, carrying sheaves with him. (Psalm 126:6)*

Introduction:

Throughout the Bible we see evidence both directly written and indirectly implied that God plants many seeds in the lives of men and women. We also see that He instructs us to sow seeds and cautions that if we sow bad seeds, we will not reap pleasant things. Conversely, God makes it very clear that if we sow good, we will reap great things.

In this chapter we will focus on:

• Components of Holy Seeds vs. Unholy Seeds

• How seeds are planted

• Conditions necessary for effective, long-term growth of the seed

Definitions:

Natural Seed

—noun

1. the fertilized, mature ovule of a flowering plant, containing an embryo or rudimentary plant.
2. the germ or propagative source of anything: *the seeds of discord.*
3. Offspring; progeny

-verb

4. to sow (a field, lawn, etc.) with seed
5. to sow or scatter with seed
6. to place, introduce, etc., esp. in the hope of increase or profit: *to seed a lake with trout.*

Spiritual Seed

—noun

1. The word of God
2. Faith
3. A substance or being planted; Beginnings of one of God's or Satan's plans
4. Sons of the Kingdom of God (Matthew 13:3)

—verb

5. to sow spiritual seed.
6. to place, introduce, etc., esp. in the hope of spiritual growth.

Scripture Study: Panted lanted in the Word

Types of Seed

The Bible discusses two types of seed that can be planted, or sown. The first is Holy seed and includes only that which is good or ordained by God. These seeds are primarily formed out of God's faithfulness and love for mankind and are ultimately purposed for His glory. There are many different positive attributes and Christ-like behaviors that can grow in our life and all, if successfully cultivated, will lead to an abundant harvest with the Fruits of the Spirit (Galatians 5:22). In contrast, unholy seed will produce nothing but despair and destruction (Galatians 6:8).

Holy Seeds

- Holy seeds are rich in <u>faithfulness</u>.

- Holy seeds are rich in <u>love</u>.

Unholy Seeds

- Unholy seeds are rich in <u>sin</u>.

- Unholy seeds are rich in <u>destructiveness</u>.

<u>How seed is planted</u>

- Seeds are planted by <u>God</u>.

The first evidence of God "planting" is found in Genesis 2:8 with the scripture "*Now the LORD God had planted a garden in the east, in Eden; and there he put the man he had formed.*" You'll notice that God could have simply said, "Let there be a garden" in the same manner that He created the basics of all things created in the first seven days, but He didn't do that. God *chose* to plant the Garden. That implies a greater reason than just having a garden appear. Why did He take the time to plant it? Perhaps because it was the place He would put man, whom He created for His pleasure and whom He loved.

Later in the Old Testament we can see further evidence of God purposefully planting a seed. Numbers 24:6 discusses aloes planted by the Lord. I find it comforting and very interesting that of all of the things that Moses might have said God planted, He used aloe as the specific thing planted. Even in biblical times, aloe was known to be medicinal and healing, and this particularly reminds me that God has planted healing in my life and will do the same for others. Through our growth journey with Him, we find that by His hand, we no longer suffer from the things we once did.

What is God referred to in John 15:1? Why do you think He is described this way?

_____

There are many reasons why God might plant a seed. What are the reasons cited in Isaiah 60:21 and Isaiah 61:11? _____

_____

Read Matthew 6:26, which offers proof that we do not need to sow our own seed for nourishment, but rather can rely on God to feed us. What specific proof does this verse offer?

_____

Like most Psalms, Psalm 92:12-14 was written based upon historical events in the Old Testament (specifically about Abraham and Sarah), but also makes a statement in general for all believers of all times. What promise do these verses offer to the righteous who are planted in the house of the Lord?

_____

_____

While God plants many seeds in our lives exclusively by His hand, sometimes He plants seeds using others.

Who did God use to help with the seed planted in 1 Corinthians 3:6? _____

As you can see, God used not only one person, but two when He made plans in Corinth. This verse refers to God instructing the first person to plant the seeds of the Gospel there and the second person to come behind the first reinforcing the gospel message. As a result, there was much church growth in this city. But as we see in the context of this verse, even though God used two others to plant and water the seed, they knew they were not responsible for any glory. It is God alone who should receive glory in our lives for it is only He who is capable of any growth within us or others.

• Seeds can be and are planted by <u>Satan</u>, either directly or through <u>society</u>.

Throughout the Bible, there are countless descriptions in many different books about God's dismay over the sinful behaviors of his chosen people which can clearly be related to seeds planted by both Satan and society. Frequently, these verses attribute the lack bearing fruit as a result of the bad seed and/or impure soil conditions. Let's explore a few of these examples.

According to Isaiah 5:1-2, what was the resulting harvest of the one who planted the vineyard?

_____

According to Amos 5:11, why would the owner of the vineyard not drink its wine?

_____

What message does this offer us today?

_____

In the above example, the owner of the vineyard was reaping what he had sown as is consistent with God's Word in Galatians 6:7. This topic is mentioned multiple times throughout the Bible as a warning from God not to sow negative seeds. In contrast, God also tells us in the Bible what happens when we plant positive seeds. As we study how seeds are planted, it's important not to miss the value in knowing what can be planted and the resulting harvest from each of these seeds.

Read the following verses and then write down what you sow and reap according to scripture.

Hosea 10:12:

If you sow _____, *you will reap* _____.

Hosea 10:13:

If you sow _____, *you will reap* _____.

Job 4:8:

If you sow _____, *you will reap* _____.

Psalm 126:5:

If you sow _____, *you will reap* _____.

Proverbs 11:18:

If you sow _____, *you will reap* _____.

Proverbs 22:8:

If you sow _____, *you will reap* _____.

2 Corinthians 9:6:

If you sow _____, *you will reap* _____.

If you sow _____, *you will reap* _____.

Galatians 6:8:

If you sow _____, *you will reap* _____.

If you sow _____, *you will reap* _____.

James 3:8:

If you sow _____, *you will reap* _____.

Effective Growth of Seed

- Seeds need to be sown in fertile soil

  One of the favored parallels in the Bible is a parable told by Jesus about sowing seeds. We briefly looked at this parable in chapter one, but will return to it now for a deeper study. Through this parable, Jesus teaches us about sowing in great detail as it relates to our relation to the word of God.

  This parable is told in three of the four gospels and although we could use any of the versions for this study, we will use the one from the book of Luke. If you would like to read the other gospel versions, they can be found in Matthew 13:1-23 and Mark 4:1-20.

  Read Luke 8:4-15, then answer the following questions.

  What happened to the seed that was thrown on the path?

  _____

  What meaning did Jesus explain for this part of the parable?

  _____

  _____

  What happened to the seed that was scattered on the rock?

  _____

  What meaning did Jesus explain for this part of the parable?

  _____

  _____

  What happened to the seed that was sown among the thorns?

  _____

  What meaning did Jesus explain for this part of the parable?

  _____

  _____

And finally as a review, what happened to the seed that was sown among good soil?

_____

What meaning did Jesus explain for this part of the parable?

_____

_____

- Seeds need right conditions to spout.

  Ecclesiastes 11:6 instructs us to sow our seed in the morning, and at evening to not let our hands be idle, for we do not know which will succeed, whether this or that, or whether both will do equally well. What point do you think Solomon was trying to make when he wrote this verse?

  _____

  _____

  _____

  _____

  _____

  _____

  _____

  From the previous chapter, what soil conditions can you identify that are necessary for optimal growth of the good seed?

  _____, _____, and _____

  When God plants a seed, is the seed always destined to bear lots of fruit? Read the following verses to find out then write down a few modern reasons why a seed planted by God might not bear fruit today.

  I had planted you like a choice vine of sound and reliable stock. How then did you turn against me into a corrupt, wild vine?(James 2:21)

  The LORD Almighty, who planted you, has decreed disaster for you, because the house of Israel and the house of Judah have done evil and provoked me to anger by burning incense to Baal. (Jeremiah 11:17)

The LORD said, "Say this to him: 'This is what the LORD says: I will overthrow what I have built and uproot what I have planted, throughout the land. (Jeremiah 45:4)

Therefore, get rid of all moral filth and the evil that is so prevalent and humbly accept the word planted in you, which can save you. (James 1:21)

_____

_____

_____

_____

_____

_____

*   Seeds need strong root system to become anchored and thrive.

The roots are the first things to grow in a seed in order to help the seed become anchored as you can see in the picture below. This is a wonderful reminder that God is our anchor long before we grow and certainly long before we bear fruit. As Romans 11:18 says, **You do not support the root, but the root supports you**.

Now look at the following picture. What do you note about the roots as compared to the plant?

_____

Reread Luke 8:13. What does this verse say is responsible for roots not forming which would mean there is no anchor present?

_____

The word "testing" used in this scripture comes from the Greek word *"perasmos"* which has a double meaning as both trial and temptation. For the purpose of this verse, God used this word to signify that we are faced with trials from Him intended to make us stand and temptation from Satan intended to make us fall. Both are part of the testing because both require an unwavering belief to successfully endure and grow roots. In fact, the root word for both testimony and testing are the same because out of our testing comes our true testimony to the amazing grace of God. Remember this as you are facing one of these great tests in your life and do not lose faith. If you can out-believe your testing period, roots will form and a great harvest will await you.

Relatable Bible Figure

For this section's study of a relatable Bible figure, we will focus on Abraham who is listed in the Hall of Faith for his belief that God would make him a father. His time of believing surely outlasted his testing period and he was eternally blessed. In fact, Abraham was designated by God to provide the seed for all mankind.

In Genesis 15, God promised Abraham that his seed would outnumber the stars. And as noted in our previous chapter Abraham believed the Lord and God credited his belief as righteousness. Abraham subsequently received many blessings, one of which was to become a father to Isaac after he thought he and Sarah would never bear children, but another was a promise God made to Abraham and his seed to make them a great nation.

According to Galatians 3:6-7, those who believe God just like Abraham believed are considered what?

_____

As children of Abraham, what does Galatians 3:9 say we will receive because of our faith?

_____

According to Galatians 3:14, how do we receive the blessings given to Abraham? What blessings will we receive by faith?

_____

_____

Who does Paul clarify the seed represents in God's promise to Abraham in Galatians 3:16? _____

According to Galatians 3:21, who is an offspring of Abraham's seed?

_____

How does Galatians 3:21 describe those who are of Abraham's seed?

_____

Think for a moment on the fact that God had you and me in mind when He told Abraham that his seed would outnumber the stars. He knew that this seed would be spread from Generation to Generation, not genetically, but spiritually and would produce a large kingdom of believers to fill up the gates of heaven. It's a wonderful thought that God's plan for us started so many years ago and will end in such an incredibly wonderful way.

As we conclude this study of the scripture, read I Corinthians 15:35-44 and the ultimate promise that it holds for believers in Christ. What is this ultimate promise?

_____

_____

To summarize what we've discussed this session, review the following chart to help you cross-reference the different seed types and soil types as it relates to spiritual growth.

Soil Type	Pure	Impure	Pure	Impure
Seed Type	Holy	Holy	Unholy	Unholy
Growth	Incredible Growth with strong roots; Plant yields abundant fruit.	Stunted Growth with shallow roots; Plant withers and produces no fruit.	Impossible combination. Soil is no longer pure if unholy seeds are scattered in it.	Growth of Destruction; Weeds choke out any remnants of good.

Blessed Assurances

- Our God is a Faithful and Loving God known for generously sprinkling seeds.
- When God's seeds fall on fertile soil and sprout, great blessings emerge.
- If you allow spiritual roots to form in your life, you will be securely anchored.
- In your Christian walk you will be tested, but with hope, faith, and trust, you will receive abundant blessings which will turn your test into a testimony.
- If your time of believing outlasts your time of testing, you will reap a 100-fold harvest.
- If you belong to Christ, you are a promised heir to the Kingdom of God.

Fertilize Yourself:

Reflect on the seeds that God has previously planted in your life and think about how those seeds grew. These may include relationships, divine appointments, directives, etc. Make a list of all of the glorious things for which you can express gratitude to God as you reflect on His faithfulness.

_____

_____

_____

_____

_____

_____

_____

_____

_____

_____

_____

_____

_____

_____

_____

_____

Chapter Three: Living Water

Foundation Scripture:

> **_I (God) will send down showers in season; there will be showers of blessing._** **_(Ezekiel 34:26)_**

Notice that in the foundation scripture for this section, God makes two definite statements: 1.) He _will_ send down showers and 2.) There _will_ be showers of blessing. God didn't use might or may or even could, but instead, He wanted to make it very clear that He is in charge of providing the showers and the blessings and that it is his absolute will that it be done.

Now notice a second thing that God says to us in this scripture. He notes that He will send down showers, specifically showers of blessing, _in season_. This lets us know that although it is His full intention to provide blessings, those blessings will come on his timetable and not ours. This is to provide for our optimal growth and that is what we will study in this chapter.

Definitions:

Physical Water

1. A clear, colorless, odorless, and tasteless liquid H_2O, essential for most plant and animal life and the most widely used of all solvents.
2. A particular quantity or body of water
   a. the water occupying a flowing in a particular bed.
   b. a quantity or depth of water adequate for some purpose (as navigation)
   c. a band of seawater abutting on the land of a particular sovereignty and under control of that sovereignty
   d. water supply
3. Travel or transportation on water (i.e. we went by water)
4. The level of water at a particular state of the tide
5. A pharmaceutical preparation made with water
6. Amniotic fluid
7. A distilled fluid
8. A watery fluid (as tears, urine, or sap) formed or circulating in a living body
9. The degree of clarity and luster of a precious stone
10. Degree of excellence (ie. a scholar of first water)

Spiritual Water

1. Of the natural element, frequently used in the gospels
2. A material resource necessary for life
3. Living Water, essential for an abundantly fruitful life
4. The Holy Spirit
5. The Word of God
6. The elements that flowed from Christ's side on the cross after His death
7. Of the truth conveyed by baptism, this being the expression, not the medium, the symbol, not the cause, of the believer's identification with Christ in HIs death, burial, and resurrection.
8. Blessings rained down upon believers according to God's good will and purpose

Scripture Study: Saturated in the Word

Water from Above

Our foundation scripture this week talks about waiting for the season when God will shower us with blessings. What does Hosea 10:12 say we should do during the time that we wait?

_____

How many showers does Joel 2:23 say God will send in His seasons?

_____

Just as Ezekiel penned God's quote about showering blessings in our foundation passage above, many other authors throughout many varying times of the Bible have used the description of rain to describe the blessings that come from above. Why? Because God is perfect and through that perfection, He is consistent in all things at all times. You'll find this throughout the Bible in countless topics and themes. Through His breath, or inspiration, the entire Bible was written. It would only make sense that each book in the Great Book would flow together like a seamless quilt to cover us with His majestic greatness. A patchwork quilt just wouldn't have had the same effect. So for this section of our study, let's focus on one of those seamless areas: God's rain.

Read Isaiah 45:8. What does God command to happen?

_____

What does this mean specific to your own personal situation?

_____

Zachariah 10:1 is a wonderful passage of hope. Who does the scripture say God gives plants of the field to after He gives showers of rain?

_____

What do Genesis 24:35, Numbers 24:7, Job 36:26-28, Psalm 65:9-11, Psalm 68:9, Psalm 78:20, Joshua 17:14, and 1 Timothy 1:14 have in common?

_____

If we pause to reflect on the meaning of the word "abundantly", we will see that God provides for us "more than adequately, over-sufficiently, and in abounding quantity." We should find much comfort in knowing how great His planned provisions are for us. Along with this, we should seek to understand why He provides so abundantly.

But what does that water really do? Let's dive into that now.

Effects of water

* Water Fills

    More than any other characteristic of the Living Water, the filling quality abounds throughout the pages of the Bible.

    Read Psalm 65:9 below and circle all of the verbs used in this passage.
    You care for the land and water it;
    you enrich it abundantly.
    The streams of God are filled with water
    to provide the people with grain,
    for so you have ordained it.

    Note in the verbs that are circled that God cares, waters, enriches, fills, provides, and finally ordains. More specifically, He fills in order to provide for a need.

Read the following scriptures and identify what you can be filled with by the hand of God as evidenced by what God has filled in others:

Exodus 31:2-4: _____

Exodus 40:34 and Numbers 14:20-22: _____

Deuteronomy 34:8-10 and Luke 2:40: _____

Job 8:21 and Psalm 126:2: _____

Psalm 4:7: _____

Psalm 16:11, Psalm 126:3, Acts 2:28, and Acts 14:17: _____

Psalm 65:54 and Psalm 107:9: _____

Psalm 71:8: _____

Psalm 72:19: _____

Psalm 119:64: _____

Isaiah 33:5: _____

Habakkuk 2:14: _____

Matthew 5:6: _____

Luke 1:15, Acts 13:52, Luke 1:41, and Luke 1:67: _____

Romans 15:13: _____

Ephesians 3:19: _____

Philippians 1:11: _____

Colossians 1:9: _____

1 Peter 1:8: _____

Finally, as we conclude the section on God's filling, let's read some verses that summarize God's filling power.

What does Ephesians 1:22-23 say Christ fills and how?

_____

What does Ephesians 3:19-20 say will happen when you allow God's love to form roots in your life and know this love that surpasses knowledge?

_____

Spend a few moments in reflection about the filling properties of God and how, when He fills you to the measure, you will have no tiny crevice… absolutely no hidden space within you…that is not touched by the fullness of Him, His love, and His power. It is a fullness that is complete and lacking nothing. And when you are filled with His fullness, you too will be complete and lacking nothing if you allow God's love to form deep roots in your life. It's a simple choice. Open up your heart to be filled today!

• Water Quenches

Our Christian souls are designed to have a thirst that seeks quenching. God designed each of us with this thirst so that He can offer the assurance of His quenching presence. Without God, we would continually dwell in a dry, parched land where there can be no fruitfulness with no hope or assurance. David is one who biblically offers such assurances as he specifically wrote of his thirst in numerous Psalms. He certainly knew thirst from personal experience when he wrote the following in Psalm 63:1: "O God, you are my God, earnestly I seek you; my soul thirsts for you, my body longs for you, in a dry and weary land where there is no water." Later, David confirms again from personal experience that God quenches his thirst when he wrote with certainty in Psalm 107 "for He satisfies the thirst and fills the hungry with good things…and turns rivers into a desert, flowing springs into thirsty ground." Notice what David states that God gave him in response to thirst…not just a drink of water, but instead He gave him abundant water. Abundance! Yes, abundant water for abundant fruitfulness we are seeking!

What confirmation does Isaiah 41:17-18 offer? What reassurance does verse 8 offer you? (read through verse 20).

_____

_____

_____

What other assurances does the Bible provide? Read the following scriptures and note the detail of these blessed assurances.

Isaiah 55:1 _____

John 4:14: _____

John 6:35: _____

John 7:37-38: _____

Revelation 21:6: _____

- Water Cleanses

In the same way that David asked God to quench his thirst, he also asked God to wash away all of his iniquity and cleanse him from his sin (Psalm 51:2). God not only washed David, but He cleansed many others. Because God made the same promise made to all mankind through His son Jesus, you and I can have our sins washed away, as well.

Read Titus 3:3-8 which describes mankind being full of sin. How does this verse say we are saved from this sin?

_____

- *What act is symbolic of our cleansing rebirth?* _____

According to Psalm 51:7, how clean can God make you?

_____

What do the following scriptures say that God cleans from us?

Ezekiel 36:25:

_____

Hebrews 9:14 & Hebrews 10:22:

_____

Jeremiah 33:8:

_____

I Corinthians 6:9-11:

_____

How do Ezekiel 36:25 and Hebrews 10:22 say God washes us?

_____

Why do you think God "sprinkles" us instead of drenching us with water to make us clean? The answer actually dates back to the Old Testament when sprinkling using blood, water, and oil was an essential part of the act of sacrifice. The sprinkling of the blood represented the covenant between God and the people (Exodus 24:6-8) and to provide purification from sins (Lev 4). Today, God makes that same covenant with us through His son, Jesus.

Now reflect on the second part of Ezekiel 36:25. Think about things that are pure like the water God uses to cleanse us. Are pure things not flawless, perfect, and much more valuable than anything else we can receive? Because God's water is so flawless, perfect, and valuable, it can serve to meet each and every one of our cleansing needs, non-cleansing needs, and even needs we might not have recognized that we had. In His perfection, He can wash away any stains from any age including those that have been set in by heated arguments or heated passions from long ago. And His water is so powerful that it can wash out all of the negatives from our soil if you allow ourselves a little sprinkle. Do you have any dirty laundry or extra baggage in your life that could use a good cleaning? Today is the perfect wash day to cleanse everything to make you new again. All you have to do is seek Him and it will be done.

- Water Refreshes

Who do Psalm 68:9 and Jeremiah 31:25 say God refreshes? _____

What do Genesis 27:29, Hosea 14:5-6, Zechariah 8:12, and Deuteronomy 33:13 have in common?

_____

Did you know that dew is regarded as a symbol of refreshing? When we review the properties of dew to understand why God created it, we see why it is referred to this way. Scientifically, typical dewy nights are considered to be calm because the wind transports nocturnally warmer air from higher levels to the cooler surface. Dew does not gather while there is heat or wind. The temperature must fall, the wind cease, and the air come to a point of coolness and rest. Dew has no need to form during a storm because the moisture is already there. Instead, dew falls during dry times which nourishes the vegetation that otherwise would die. Thus, God provides that even during the calm, dry periods, plants can still be refreshed.

Spiritually, dew occurs during calm nights when communion is at a minimum as a way for God to provide continual watering. Dew provides sense of renewal each morning. Have you ever decided to 'sleep on' something and found much refreshing clarity in the morning? Yes, God's dew was at work. Don't forget to seek some tonight.

How else does Acts 3:19 say we can receive refreshing from the Lord?

_____

What should we do as a profession of our repentance from our previous life and acceptance of Christ as our Lord and Savior in our new spiritual life according to Acts 2:38? Why should we do this?

_____

Alterations in Water that Affect Growth

- Drought

Read the following scriptures then answer the questions below.

This is what the LORD Almighty says: "Give careful thought to your ways. Go up into the mountains and bring down timber and build the house, so that I may take pleasure in it and be honored," says the LORD. "You expected much, but see, it turned out to be little. What you brought home, I blew away. Why?" declares the LORD Almighty. "Because of my house, which remains a ruin, while each of you is busy with his own house. Therefore, because of you the heavens have withheld their dew and the earth its crops. I called for a drought on the fields and the mountains, on the grain, the new wine, the oil and whatever the ground produces, on men and cattle, and on the labor of your hands." (Haggai 1: 7-11)

The LORD will turn the rain of your land into falling dust; it will descend on you from the sky until you are destroyed. (Deuteronomy 28:24)

When the skies are shut and there is no rain, because they have sinned against You, and they pray toward this place and praise Your name, and they turn from their sins because You are afflicting them. (1 Kings 8:35)

Although he flourishes among [his] brothers, an east wind will come, a wind from the LORD rising up from the desert. His water source will fail, and his spring will run dry. The wind will plunder the treasury of every precious item. (Hosea 13:16)

What do these verses have in common?

_____

Yes, these scriptures all clearly state that God can and will produce a drought upon humans. Why does He allow a drought to happen? He allows it when we have distanced ourselves from His living water in the same manner that the ground is in a state of drought when it is without water. We essentially create our own drought by wandering away from God and the path He has chosen for us.

Based upon scripture, we know that God leads us beside still waters and further will allow springs of living water to flow from within us if we follow his path. Yet often times, when we are following the path that God has carefully chosen for us, we begin to stray. Why would we ever stray from the path of a loving God who is providing so well for our needs as we travel on His path? There are two reasons. First and probably the most significant is Satan. Above all other things that Satan has mastered, his skill of distracting us and tempting us is his craftiest. Most often, Satan's deception is so slight that we don't even notice when he entices us off the path and into the desert. One way he does this is to make us doubt God. Not doubt *in* God, of course, but he makes us doubt that God will answer a particular prayer and it is then our lack of faith that leads us wandering off the path. Satan also strives to make sure that we, as humans, absorb what our culture pumps into us. Our culture thrives on busyness and a focus on self. This serves to dilute the body of its spiritual water and essentially creates dehydration much like someone stranded at sea drinking salt water.

The second reason a drought occurs is because of man's free will and sinful nature. Despite God leading us in a particular direction, it's possible for man to simply take another course, perhaps one that seems less treacherous. But it's important to remember that even a treacherous journey with God is much better than an easy road without Him. Trust me, the easy road might seem smooth at first, but it won't be long until the drought will set in and your thirst will overcome you, and the only thing that will be able to grow in your life is sin. As a result, not only will you have distanced yourselves from God and his path, but the sin itself will have pulled you away from God even further.

Fortunately, however, our God is a loving and merciful God. 2 Chronicles 7 gives us a good example of this as it clarifies God's mercy on us when we are in a state of drought. Read this one carefully and thoughtfully, then answer the question that follows.

If I close the sky so there is no rain…and My people who are called by My name humble themselves, pray and seek My face, and turn from their evil ways, then I will hear from heaven, forgive their sin, and heal their land. My eyes will now be open and My ears attentive to prayer from this place. And I have now chosen and consecrated this temple so that My name may be there forever; My eyes and My heart will be there at all times. (2 Chronicles 7)

What does this verse say will cause God to heal those suffering a drought?

_____

Now comes the good part. In the first part of this scripture God said that He could cause a drought if needed, but would stop the drought if people humbled themselves and prayed to Him, turning from their evil ways. Then He moves on to note that His *eyes will be open and ears attentive to prayer.* When you are attentive to something, you are waiting for it to happen much like a new mother is attentive to the cries of her baby at night even while she sleeps. This lets us know that God is attentive to our prayers even when we are away from Him and even when we are suffering a drought. In the next line of scripture, God says that He has chosen and consecrated this temple so that his name will be there forever. If you weren't aware of it, God frequently uses the word temple as a double meaning in the Bible to refer not only to the literal temple, but also to figuratively refer to our body. In this verse, God is saying that He has chosen and consecrated our body so that His name may be there forever. If we are saved, He will forever dwell with us. In closing, He notes that His eyes and heart will be within us at all times. This means that even during the drought, God is watching us, thinking of us, loving us, and listening for our prayers because the instant the prayers happen, the living water can then begin to flow again in our lives.

In addition to droughts, we also can be in a state of dessert wilderness. When this happens it is often God allowing us to experience the dessert simply to draw nearer to Himself.

In studying the path God led the Israelites on when leading them to the Promised Land, we find that God did not take them the shortest path to the Promised Land, but instead led them to practically the furthest point away where He spoke to them on Mt. Sinai. There was great purpose in that journey through the wilderness and desert. It was there that He drew them closer to Himself and gave them experiences to prove that He was their Sustainer.

Read Isaiah 48:21. What does it say God did for those He led through the desert?

_____

This is a great reminder that God can, and will, do supernatural acts to provide us with water whenever He leads us through a barren land. If you feel you are going through a season of desert wilderness right now, be encouraged that there is purpose in this and that God's sustaining presence is always there with sustaining water for your journey.

- Storms

Just as we face droughts as an alteration in our rainfall amounts, we also encounter storms. Instead of showers of blessing, we experience torrential rains that sometimes feel like a flood. He uses these times as an opportunities to flood us with all of His greatness.

Think about the previous seasons in your life in which you faced a storm. As the storm progressed did you find yourself leaning more on God for support? As the storm cleared, how did you feel? Did you feel safe, secure and loved? Often, that's the outcome both during and after a storm.

Charles Stanley has defined six different spiritual principles that shed light on why storms occur:

1. <u>God commands our attention through cleansing.</u>
   This principle generally happens when we are not walking in God's will, which as we previously learned means that we are in a state of drought. To get our attention, God sometimes will allow a storm to form in our life which is greatly needed after dwelling in a land without water for so long. Once the storm begins, we almost certainly turn to God and depend on him much more than we did when life was smooth. And through our reliance on him, we begin to grow once again and often admit at the conclusion of the storm that the storm itself was really a good thing and the outcome was worth all of the suffering that we went through. Remember, the drought occurs when we wander from God. Because of his great love for us and desire or our nearness, He uses the storm to bring us back into his presence on the path He has planned for us.

2. <u>God wants us to walk intimately with Him in companionship.</u>
   As humans, we sometimes take our blessings for granted. We often feel safe and secure in our comfortable lifestyle and fail to make an effort to grow spiritually as a result. Oh, we might go

to church and pray, but are we really on our life's journey walking hand in hand, step by step with God? Sometimes, it takes a storm for us to realize the need for a close companionship with God. David certainly realized this when he wrote "In the shadow of your wings I will take refuge until the disaster passes by." Like David, we should view our relationship with God similar to a child who relies on a parent. Not only is the parent there to provide shelter and security from the storm, he or she is there to provide the daily bread, guidance, teaching, showers of love upon the child, and any other need that might arise. That, too, is what we can expect from our Lord and we can only get that if we are in continual companionship with Him.

3. <u>God is reshaping us to the likeness of His Son by conformity.</u>
   We have a tendency in life to often conform to society which can form holes and jagged edges in our lives. God wants us to be more like Jesus than the world and thus sends storms to help soften our furrows and level our edges. Conforming to Christ means that we behave in the same manner that Christ did with the same virtues that He modeled and taught. By conforming to Christ, we are filling our soil with needed purity. In contrast, when we have negative or sinful behaviors in our life, our soil is corrupt and much less likely to grow good fruit. As we learned in the first chapter of our study, even something like fear can and does inhibit our spiritual growth and fruitfulness as it does not match the behavior that Jesus would have exhibited in the same situation. So through the storm, God helps us to identify some of these behaviors and helps to reshape us to wash them from our lives through the overwhelming presence of His living water.

4. <u>God wants to do something special with us through comfort.</u>
   I have come to realize that this is one of the reasons for the infertility I suffered years ago. God will often use storms to grow Christians who will go forth and provide comfort to those going through the same experience. He needs people who are not only sensitive and compassionate to the situation, but also those who can confirm with certainty that God stayed with them in the midst of the storm and provided significant blessings upon enduring the storm. As humans, we need that type of validation in our lives and God realizes that. He knows that our faith can be enhanced greatly through the testimony of someone who's already suffered whatever the storm might be and survived. And so, in order to allow this to be possible, some people simply have to endure a storm so they can live to tell about it.

5. <u>God helps us determine what we believe about Him through convictions.</u>
   Simply put, we are being put to the test. In times of trouble, our true faith in God as our savior is exposed. We are either found to be doubtful and questioning unanswered prayers or we are found to carry a blind confidence that God has a plan, is in control, and will save us from the storm. Storms reveal our doubts, but they also deepen our dependence. When life is sunny and calm, we often lose the dependence because we have no need for refuge. But during the storm, trusting in Him teaches us how present, powerful, protective and providing He is when we need Him the most. We emerge as a changed person, more trusting and faithful when the next storm appears on life's horizon. And as faith is strengthened, the soil is fertilized and spiritual growth is enhanced leading to the fruitfulness we so desire in our lives.

6. <u>God wants to rescue us from our disobedience through change.</u>
    At times some of us not only wander away and accidentally find ourselves in a desert, we intentionally go to their in an act of total rebellion against God. Perhaps you feel God leading you in a path that you don't really want to take. Many have experienced this when God was beckoning them to return to church or to return to the Word. Their absolute refusal to follow God's command leads to torrential storms so fierce at times that the one rebelling is blinded and helpless to everything but the presence of God. Subsequently, the person has no option but to turn to God for help and, as always, our loving, merciful God will rescue him and carry him safely back home.

Did you notice that in each of the above lists, God teaches us through his ability to rescue us? God did the same thing in Matthew 8. Read verses 23-27 and answer the following:

Did Jesus rescue the disciples from the storm because of their faith?

_____

What was the disciple's response?

_____

While we might want to figure out why God is sending us through a storm, it really isn't necessary. The necessary part is that we allow him to rescue us and credit Him and only Him with all of the details of our salvation.

<u>Receiving the Living Water</u>

Hosea 6:3 tells us that God will come to us like spring rain. What must we do to receive this rain?

_____

Who does John 4:13 specifically say gives Living Water? _____

How does Matthew 7:7-8 say we receive from Jesus?

_____

_____

How does Matthew 7:9-11 describe our relationship to God and his giving?

_____

_____

That sounds simple enough, doesn't it? Just ask God and –poof- you have everything your heart desires, right? Not right. There is a serious flaw in your thinking if that's what you believe, but many Christians believe just that. We tend to want to use the Bible conveniently for our own interpretation from a single verse and not look at the broader picture. If we only read Matthew 7:7 and didn't apply what we know to be true about God, then we could easily interpret this to be the resemblance of God as a Genie in a Magic Lamp. But we know this is not the case. We know this because of the unanswered prayers that seem to pile up in some of our lives. So the question is…if He doesn't grant each request to everyone who asks, why not?

There are actually at several reason why a prayer might not be answered. The first we've already alluded to in our study: It's simply not the right time. I waited five years with prayers that were seemingly unanswered because the time was not right. I often wonder where Emily would be right now if God had granted my prayer and given me a biological child early on in my times of trouble. Every time I think this, I am filled with so much appreciation to God for not answering that prayer. He knew when she would be born and He knew that I had to wait. And in the end when all of His glorious fruition was laid before me, I realized that I'd never had an unanswered prayer. It was simply a delayed prayer awaiting fulfillment. Remember, when your time of believing outlasts your time of testing, you'll be greatly blessed. I know it's difficult some times, but if you patiently await his timing with hope, faith, and trust, your mind will be blown away with what God has in store for you.

The next reason why God might not answer a prayer is because the prayer isn't consistent with God's will for our lives. We are saying not *thy* will be done, but *my* will be done. I prayed for several years for a pregnancy. That didn't happen. Over the course of the years, however, my prayers changed from 'pregnancy' to 'child' and that's when I finally emerged from the darkness on to the path that God had planned for me all along. When my prayers were consistent with what God wanted in my life, they were answered. Had I continued an unwavering prayer for pregnancy and failed to seek His light, I would still be pining away after something that would never come and He would never have received His glory. Why did God choose adoption over pregnancy for me? He has revealed many reasons to me including His divine will that I be in this study with you today. Had I not endured the storm and the incredible clearing that still leaves me in awe, it would never have been possible. Yes, God has plans for us and a will that He will assuredly bring to completion. In the next chapter as we discuss seeking God's light in your life, we'll delve deeper into how you can seek to know His will.

Another related reason why God might not answer a prayer can be found in James 4:3.

What does this verse say is a primary reason for unanswered prayers?

_____

If you have the wrong motivation for a prayer, such someone who has a love for money praying for God to allow him to win the lottery, that prayer simply won't be answered. Our God is a jealous God and will refuse to subsidize any prayer that takes away focus from him. Giving someone who idolizes money the winnings of a lottery would certainly further remove the man from God's presence and God will simply not allow that. The same goes with abundant sin in our lives. Just like a parent doesn't reward a defiant child, God will not reward someone who is rebelling against him. To do so would go against the very nature of His justified authority over our lives and would certainly defeat his goal to command praise from his believers.

Finally, God might not answer a prayer if He feels it is not given in full devotion and seriousness. He commands our full attention during our time with Him and He commands that we are attentive to His Holy Spirit. When we offer our prayers weekly and weakly instead of continually and with intimate communion, we fail to pray in obedience to the command of God who instructed us to pray continually and with fervency. This truth is most applicable when we pray for wisdom, endurance, strength, and other attributes that He can give us. These things can only be acquired when we spend time with Him which demonstrates our full devotion to Him, the relationship we have with Him, and His will for our lives.

So then, how should we pray for our requests (also known as a prayer of petition or supplication) or for others (known as a prayer of intercession)? Let's look at a few verses from the Bible to find out.

Read the following scriptures to identify our instructions on how to pray:

Ephesians 6:18: _____

Colossians 4:2: _____

Mark 11:24: _____

James 1:5-8: _____

_____

Romans 12:12: _____

James 5:16-18: _____

_____

Matthew 6:5-8: _____

_____

Now I want to point out that Matthew 6 isn't saying never pray in public. There is certainly a place for public prayer in certain settings, but what it is saying is do not pray for recognition from others or offer your *personal* prayers in public. Those are to be as an intimate communication with God that is only offered to God and not for the intent of having others hear you.

1 Thessalonians 5:16-18: _____

What do you think it means to pray continually? Is it possible to live in a state of continual prayer yet accomplish other simultaneous tasks? The key to understanding how his is possible is to understand the definition of prayer which is a spiritual communion with God, or communicating intimately with Him. With practice, communicating intimately with God will become just as continuous as it is if you are in the physical presence of another human with whom you are intimately close. Because of the many different types of prayer...including prayers of thanksgiving and adoration, prayers of petition, prayers of intercession, prayers of praise, and prayers of repentance... there is always something new to talk about with our Lord and Savior in the moments of life rather than storing everything up for a bedtime prayer. These on-the-spot moments of communion with God are highly effective in helping us to grow spiritually by keeping us constantly fertilized by His presence.

Finally, we come to the end of our prayer and say "in Jesus name Amen". Why did Jesus command us to pray in His name?

John 14:13-14: _____

John 15:16: _____

John 16:24: _____

Colossians 3:17: _____

John 14:6 : _____

Does John 16:26 say that we pray in Jesus name so that He will ask the Father on our behalf?

_____

$\mathcal{R}$elatable $\mathcal{B}$ible $\mathcal{F}$igure:

The Bible contains many short stories about Jesus' encounters with others during his time on earth. One of the greatest is the story of His encounter with the woman at the well. This story stands out not only because of the conversation that Jesus had with her, but also because the encounter even occurred. You see, in those days Jewish people did not associate with Samaritans, so in doing so Jesus demonstrated another principle - doing what was right according to God rather than what was expected of him by society. Today, we still have a lot to learn from this principle and from the encounter itself, which contains some vital wisdom about Jesus as living water.

Read John 4:1-26. Where did Jesus say the living water comes from and what did He say it would do?

_____

_____

How did the woman at the well know it was really Jesus speaking to her?

_____

Thankfully, we all can be met at the well by the Messiah. He already knows everything in our past, but still chooses by His amazing grace to give us His living water anyway. Keep your eyes open and seek Him when you are thirsty at the well. True to His promise, you will never thirst again.

ℛeflection:

The scriptures in today's study are just as real and applicable today as they were in the times they were written. Take a minute to reflect on how a few of these scriptures can be applied directly to you and rewrite them as if they were originally meant only for you. The first one is done for you as an example.

- *You care for the land and water it; You enrich it abundantly. The stream of God are filled with water to provide the people with grain, for so you have ordained it. You drench its furrows and level its ridges; you soften it with showers and bless its crops. You crown the year with your bounty, and your carts overflow with abundance. – Psalm 65:9-11*

  You care for me and water me; You enrich me abundantly. The streams of God are filled with water to provide me with all I need, for so you have ordained it. You drench my furrows and level my ridges; You soften me with showers and bless me. You crown the year with your bounty, and your carts overflow with abundance.

- *They will neither hunger nor thirst, nor will the dessert heat or sun beat upon them. He who has compassion on them will guide them and lead them beside springs of water. – Isaiah 49:10*

  _____

  _____

  _____

  _____

  _____

- *The Lord with guide you always; he will satisfied your needs in a sun-scorched land and will strengthen your frame. You will be like a well-watered garden, like a spring whose waters never fail. – Isaiah 58:11*

  _____

  _____

  _____

  _____

- *But his delight is in the law of the Lord and on his law he meditates day and night. He is like a tree planted by streams of water, which yields its fruit in season and whose leaf does not wither. Whatever he does prospers.-Psalm 1:2-4*

_____

_____

_____

_____

_____

- *How priceless is your unfailing love! Both high and low among men find refuge in the shadow of your wings. They feast on the abundance of your house; you give them drink from your river of delights. For with you is the fountain of life; in your light we see light. - Psalm 36:7-9*

_____

_____

_____

_____

_____

*F*ertilize yourself this week:

When we are filled with anything that is not of Christ, including fleshly things of the world and of self, then we cannot be completely filled with things of the Spirit. Take some time this week to reflect on the things in your life that may keep you from being filled to the measure with all the Lord wants to fill you with! Make a point to start each day in prayer asking God to identify and empty you of those things, then allow yourself to be refilled continually with His Holy Presence. Practice continual prayer by communing with God in intimate communication all throughout the day. Talk to him about all of your frustrations, joys, pleasures, and even the things in life that you find humorous. Share personal moments with Him as you read the Word, listen to praise and worship music, or have lunch with a dear Christian friend. Experience the many wonderful ways that God can fill you with Himself, and allow your inner self to be nurtured to abundant growth through the Living Water that flows within you!

Chapter Four: Abundant Light

Foundation Scripture

"I will lead the blind by ways they have not known, along unfamiliar paths I will guide them; I will turn the darkness into light before them and make the rough places smooth. These are the things I will do; I will not forsake them".
(Isaiah 42:16)

Introduction

We are all blind to something at some time in our life. Often times, we are even blind to many things at once and certainly travel along many unfamiliar paths. I certainly did when I embarked on my journey through infertility. The journey for me started out so innocently. After all, I had easily conceived two children already, so a third, I confidently thought, would be a breeze. But as the weeks turned into months and the months into years, my husband and I had to acknowledge that we were in a very foreign place. For us, the biggest question was not "How did we get here?" but "How do we get out of it?" Fortunately, God led us to seek Himself early on in this journey, and He not only walked the path with us, He held the light that guided us along the path to where we now reside today. He not only brought to light the answer to our question (which for us was *in vitro* fertilization vs. adoption); He also went out like a shepherd herding His sheep and led us to the exact place He wanted us. Even more incredibly, He shed his light on us and also on an incredible young couple in

Tennessee and led us all together in a set of unmistakable divinely-inspired events. It was a match literally made in heaven. And the warmth of His light continues to shine upon us to this very day.

Definitions

Physical Light

-noun

1. something that makes things visible or affords illumination
2. the state of being visible, exposed to view, or revealed to public notice or knowledge spiritual illumination or awareness
3. enlightenment
4. mental insight
5. understanding

- verb

6. to cause (the face, surroundings, etc.) to brighten, esp. with joy, animation, or the like
7. "bring to light" = to discover or reveal

Spiritual Light

-noun

1. Christ as the Light of the World who makes things visible or affords illumination
2. the state of being visible, exposed to view, or revealed to public notice or knowledge
3. spiritual illumination or awareness
4. enlightenment
5. mental insight
6. understanding

- verb

7. to cause (the face, surroundings, etc.) to brighten, esp. with joy, animation, or the like
8. "bring to light" = to discover or reveal
9. Spirit of Knowledge, Wisdom, Understanding and Council as those are attributes that illuminate us from within.

Scripture Study: Illuminating the Word

Our foundation scripture for this chapter notes that God will be the light for our path and will make the rough spots smooth.

To what scripture from the previous study is this passage similar?

_____

What assurance does that give you?

_____

Throughout the Bible, there are many references to God providing light for illumination, or to make things visible. It is the most common reference to light in the Bible and first occurs very early in the Word. In fact, of all the scriptures about light in the Bible, everyone is most familiar with the first one in Genesis 1:3 "And God said, 'Let there be light,' and there was light." The sole purpose of this light in this context was to provide illumination for the earth. But if you've ever paid attention to the happenings on each day of creation, you might have noticed that although light was created on day one, the sun wasn't created until day four. That's because the sun isn't the provider of light; God is the provider of light.

Another early example of God as light is seen in the book of Exodus in the account of God helping the Israelites out of Egypt. To guide them, God "by day led them with a pillar of cloud, and by night with a pillar of fire to give them light on the way they were to take (Nehemiah 9:12)." Then, after He led them to safety, God had Moses construct the Ark of the Covenant, which again held strong evidence of God as light. He instructed Moses to create the lamp stand, upon which seven candles would light a sacred portion of the Ark of the Covenant. Were you aware that God had Moses build it out of hammered gold so that the light from the candles, reflecting on the gold, would produce brilliance? Many scholars believe that this structure was meant to represent, in prophesy, Jesus as "the Light of the world." God also had Moses create it with a design of almond buds and blossoms, which represent spiritual blessings in the present and future fruit to come. Why the almond? It was the first tree to blossom in the spring and would remind people of resurrection of new life! And, of course, the design of the lamp stand having one main stand with six branches ties in perfectly as it was planned with John 15:5 when Jesus said, "I am the vine, you are the branches." Many scholars also believe that the seven lamps that sit upon the branches of the lamp stand represent the following seven Spirits of God: 1.) Spirit of the LORD, 2.) Spirit of wisdom, 3.) Spirit of understanding, 4.) Spirit of counsel, 5.) Spirit of power, 6.) Spirit of knowledge, and 7.) Spirit of the fear of the Lord. All seven refer to the powerful attributes of God, which enlighten us.

There are many other references in the Bible to God as light. Let's look at a few of these examples together and examine how the same illuminating light is still present today. Since many of the references that we will study come from the book of Psalms, let's begin by taking a detailed look at the Psalms and their presence in the Bible.

It might surprise you to know that it has been determined that each and every possible human emotion is contained in the book of Psalms. They were originally written as songs to provide a wonderful reminder to the people collectively that God is a faithful provider. Today, we still acknowledge the same assurance when we read them, not only because of the stories of old as told in the Bible, but because we, too, have our own stories to tell that fit one or more Psalms perfectly. (Isn't it so awesome that God inspired the Bible to be so perfectly applicable for the span of many millennia?)

Here are some facts about the Psalms that you might not know.

- They were written primarily by David, but were also penned by other authors during a time span from 1490 BC. to 444 BC.

- The Psalms are categorized into five hymn books, each with a specific message.

- Each of the five hymn books corresponds to the first five books of the Bible in order, or the Pentateuch.

- Each individual "chapter" is actually a hymn and is referred to in the singular form as a "Psalm."

Among the many topics discussed in the Psalms, God as living water and as light abundantly fill many of the passages as a recurrent theme by many authors. Again, just as we shouldn't be surprised that the Psalms are applicable today, we shouldn't be surprised that so many of the great biblical writers referred to God as water and light even before Jesus came to make this a formal statement. This is just another example to demonstrate the divine intervention that inspired the Bible. I find it so fascinating that you could fill a room with people and ask them to write about a general topic, and the odds of two people writing the same thing are very slim, but in the Bible, from Genesis to Revelation, the various authors all penned identical concepts and frequently used the same words. Does that thrill you as much as it does me?

Let's look at some of those thrills together as we study the properties of light found in the Bible.

- Light illuminates/makes visible

  "You, O Lord, keep my lamp burning; my God turns my darkness into light." *(Psalm 18:28)*

  "Send forth your light and your truth, let them guide me; let them bring me to your holy mountain, to the place where you dwell." *(Psalm 43:3)*

  "For you have delivered me from death and my feet from stumbling, that I may walk before God in the light of life." *(Psalm 56:13)*

  "Blessed are those who have learned to acclaim, who walk in the light of your presence." *(Psalm 89:15)*

  "Light is shed upon the righteous and joy on the upright in heart." *(Psalm 7:11)*

  "Your word is a lamp to my feet and a light for my path." *(Psalm 119:105)*

The above scriptures clearly define the role of God as a lamp providing light for the pathway. Summarize what these scriptures collectively say in one or two sentences. Remember to include to whom God provides light, how it is accomplished, and the outcome.

_____

_____

_____

- Light clarifies

Read Psalm 13. Why was David asking God to give light to his eyes?

_____

_____

David concludes Psalm 13 with confirmation of his faith in God. What does he say and why is this significant? David said that he trusts in God's unfailing love and his heart rejoices in God's salvation, noting that he will sing to the Lord because He has been good to him. It's significant because despite David's bleak outlook, he recognized that God had been good to him in the past and knew that God would again be faithful. The importance is that he knew God.

What does Ephesians 1:19 say should be enlightened and why?

_____

_____

- Light exposes

What does 1 Corinthians 4:5 say God will bring to light and expose?

_____

From the same scripture, what is the result of the exposure?

_____

According to Psalm 90:8, can we hide any of our secret sins from God? _____

- Light brightens

Read Psalm 4:6–8. What does the Psalmist imply as the outcome of the light of the Lord's face shining upon him?

_____

According to Psalm 19:8, what provides light to our eyes?

_____

Read Psalm 112. What does the Psalmist say will happen for the gracious, compassionate, and righteous man who fears the Lord and finds great delight in His command?

_____

What other promises does Psalm 112 offer? Be specific to your journey.

_____

_____

- Light provides protection

   The following scriptures clearly define the role of God as a light providing protection.

   Summarize what these scriptures collectively say by filling in the blank spaces in the two sentences below.

   "The Lord is my light and my salvation—whom shall I fear? The Lord is the stronghold of my life—of whom shall I be afraid?" (Psalm 27:1)

   "It was not by their sword that they won the land, nor did their arm bring victory; it was your right hand, your arm, and the light of your face, for you loved them." (Psalm 44:3)

   "Even in darkness light dawns for the upright for the gracious and compassionate and righteous man." (Psalm 112:4)

   "Even the darkness will not be dark to you; the light will shine like the day for the darkness is as light to you." (Psalm 139:12)

Because the Lord is my _____, my _____, and the _____ of my life, the _____ will not be _____ for me and I shall fear no one. If I am _____, _____, _____, and _____, the light will dawn for me in darkness and I will have victory because of God's right hand, His arm, and the _____ of His face because he _____ me.

For what reason does the Psalmist attribute God's continual light in our darkness in Psalm 139: 12–13?

_____

_____

Receiving God's Light

According to Psalms 119:130, what gives light?

_____

What do you think David was implying when he used the word unfolding?

_____

_____

_____

To understand completely how God's word provides light, we must first understand the three ways that God uses his word to provide us this light, which make up the doctrinal foundation on which we understand the Bible and appreciate its integrity and power.

As defined and understood the three doctrines are as follows:

1. **Doctrine of Revelation:** the supernatural act of God by which He communicated divine truths to humans that they would otherwise not know. God chose to communicate the truths through: 1.) oral communication, such as when He spoke directly to Moses; 2.) visible communication, such as that in which nature is used (i.e. Star of Bethlehem); 3.) written communication, such as when He personally wrote the Ten Commandments of the two stone tablets.

   This doctrine describes the direction in which the emerging new earth would go under God's careful guidance. All three forms of communication no longer exist and ceased to exist after Christ came to Earth because Jesus took over the role as communicator to us both directly when He was on Earth and later through the Holy Spirit after His resurrection.

2. **Doctrine of Inspiration:** the supernatural act of God wherein He directed the human authors of scripture. God used four components to accomplish this doctrine: 1.) the source of the information, the Holy Spirit, whose role was to guard the truth as it was transferred from heaven to Earth; 2.) the agent who was a human writer acting as an earthly scribe for God; 3.) the end result, which was an inerrant, completely trustworthy, once-and-for-all record given by God and thoroughly accredited; and 4.) the careful guidance by God to make sure that the human writers did not accidentally alter His Word based on their unique personalities and writing styles, so His Word would be recorded precisely.

   This doctrine also no longer exists in its active stage because the Bible is no longer being written. The Bible itself is a complete, precise, and final record, to which nothing can be added and from which nothing may be taken away. It was written by over forty authors over a span of over 1600 years, yet is written with such precision, consistency, flow, and seamlessness that it could only have been done by God's direct authority. God might inspire others to write spiritual books, but never again will man author His direct authoritative word.

3. **Doctrine of Illumination:** the supernatural influence of the Holy Spirit on those who are in the right relationship with God, so that our lives are transformed by God's power as He enables us to understand and apply God's inspired Word to our lives. As we have just studied, illumination is God's way of communicating knowledge that He wants us to know, council that He want us to receive, and wisdom about His plan and will for our lives.

This doctrine is alive and well! To this day, man continues to receive understanding from the Bible in a supernatural manner that no other book can provide. This point is included because it's important for us to understand that the Bible just isn't a collection of feel-good quotes. Instead, the Bible is supernaturally charged in a way that we only realize once we experience it and the light that accompanies it.

Because we have the Holy Spirit indwelling in us as a result of our salvation, we are assured that we will receive this illuminating light. Make no mistake … The Holy Spirit has all of the glorious power of God because He is God. Every thought you have in your head, every prayer that you pray, every disappointment you face, every tear you shed, and everything in every way about you is known by the Holy Spirit because He lives within you and is of God. It's important to understand this fact in order to truly appreciate what the Holy Spirit brings to your life.

The four defining characteristics of God imparted to the Holy Spirit that dwells within you are:

- Omnipotence—"God is all powerful." This means that He is able to accomplish powerful, supernatural acts because He contains all of the same power that God used to create the earth. Unexplained miracles of God are attributed to this characteristic. To remember this, note the root word *potent*, which means *powerful*.

- Omnipresence—"God is all present." This means that God's Spirit is ever present with us on Earth at all times and in all places. He will never leave us nor forsake us. Our bodies are the temple in which the Holy Spirit lives and where He wants to be. This attribute explains why we are able to feel filled with peace, despite hardships and troubles. To remember this one, note the root word *present*.

- Omniscience—"God is all knowing." This means that the Holy Spirit knows absolutely everything. He knows our thoughts, our sins, and even the exact number of hairs on our heads. And He also knows every bit of knowledge that can ever be known. That's why He is able to shed so much light on a particular problem with which we might be wrestling when in need of a solution. And because He already knows our destiny, He is able to provide the light necessary to guide our path as we travel there. To remember this attribute, note the root word *science*, which refers to knowledge.

- Omnibenevolence – "God is all loving." This means that God has infinite and perfect love for man. As such, it denotes that God is inherently good and merciful, and can possess absolutely no evil. Some people argue this attribute with the debate that an all-loving God would not allow people to suffer, but their arguments are unfounded. If God were to eliminate all suffering from the world, there would be no need to seek Him and no need for heaven. Instead, He allows suffering as part of this temporal world, knowing that something far better awaits all believers with His eternal glory.

Read the following scriptures and then mark the holy characteristic(s) with which each is associated.

"Wealth and honor come from you; you are the ruler of all things. In your hands are strength and power to exalt and give strength to all." (1 Chronicles 29:12)

☐ Omnipotence   ☐ Omnipresence   ☐ Omniscience   ☐ Omnibenevolence

"To God belong wisdom and power; counsel and understanding are his." (Job 12:13)

☐ Omnipotence   ☐ Omnipresence   ☐ Omniscience   ☐ Omnibenevolence

"The Spirit of the LORD will rest on him—the Spirit of wisdom and of understanding, the Spirit of counsel and of power, the Spirit of knowledge and of the fear of the LORD." (Isaiah 11:2)

☐ Omnipotence   ☐ Omnipresence   ☐ Omniscience   ☐ Omnibenevolence

"But Jesus beheld them, and said unto them, With men this is impossible; but with God all things are possible." (Matthew 19:26)

☐ Omnipotence   ☐ Omnipresence   ☐ Omniscience   ☐ Omnibenevolence

"O LORD God Almighty, who is like you? You are mighty, O LORD, and your faithfulness surrounds you." (Psalm 89:8)

☐ Omnipotence   ☐ Omnipresence   ☐ Omniscience   ☐ Omnibenevolence

"When Abram was ninety-nine years old, the LORD appeared to him and said, "I am God Almighty." (Genesis 17:1)

☐ Omnipotence   ☐ Omnipresence   ☐ Omniscience   ☐ Omnibenevolence

"For with God nothing shall be impossible." (Luke 1:37)

☐ Omnipotence   ☐ Omnipresence   ☐ Omniscience   ☐ Omnibenevolence

"Give thanks to the God of heaven, for His steadfast love endures forever." (Psalm 136:26)

☐ Omnipotence   ☐ Omnipresence   ☐ Omniscience   ☐ Omnibenevolence

"Great is our Lord and mighty in power; his understanding has no limit." (Psalm 147:5)

☐ Omnipotence   ☐ Omnipresence   ☐ Omniscience   ☐ Omnibenevolence

"Am I only a God nearby," declares the LORD, "and not a God far away? Can anyone hide in secret places so that I cannot see him?" declares the LORD. "Do not I fill heaven and earth?" declares the LORD. (Jeremiah 23:23–24)

☐ Omnipotence   ☐ Omnipresence   ☐ Omniscience   ☐ Omnibenevolence

"You are the God who performs miracles; you display your power among the peoples." (Psalm 77:14)

☐ Omnipotence   ☐ Omnipresence   ☐ Omniscience   ☐ Omnibenevolence

"They will tell of the power of your awesome works, and I will proclaim your great deeds." (Psalm 145:6)

☐ Omnipotence   ☐ Omnipresence   ☐ Omniscience   ☐ Omnibenevolence

"Lift your eyes and look to the heavens: Who created all these? He who brings out the starry host one by one, and calls them each by name. Because of his great power and mighty strength, not one of them is missing." (Isaiah 40:26)

☐ Omnipotence   ☐ Omnipresence   ☐ Omniscience   ☐ Omnibenevolence

"Ah, Sovereign LORD, you have made the heavens and the earth by your great power and outstretched arm. Nothing is too hard for you." (Jeremiah 32:17)

☐ Omnipotence   ☐ Omnipresence   ☐ Omniscience   ☐ Omnibenevolence

"By his power God raised the Lord from the dead, and He will raise us also." (1 Corinthians 6:14)

☐ Omnipotence ☐ Omnipresence ☐ Omniscience ☐ Omnibenevolence

"For the kingdom of God is not a matter of talk but of power." (1 Corinthians 4:20)

☐ Omnipotence ☐ Omnipresence ☐ Omniscience ☐ Omnibenevolence

"But we have this treasure in jars of clay to show that this all-surpassing power is from God and not from us." (2 Corinthians 4:7)

☐ Omnipotence ☐ Omnipresence ☐ Omniscience ☐ Omnibenevolence

"I pray that out of his glorious riches He may strengthen you with power through his Spirit in your inner being, so that Christ may dwell in your hearts through faith." (Ephesians 3:16)

☐ Omnipotence ☐ Omnipresence ☐ Omniscience ☐ Omnibenevolence

"I pray also that the eyes of your heart may be enlightened in order that you may know the hope to which He has called you, the riches of his glorious inheritance in the saints, and his incomparably great power for us who believe. That power is like the working of his mighty strength, which he exerted in Christ when he raised him from the dead and seated him at his right hand in the heavenly realms, far above all rule and authority, power and dominion, and every title that can be given, not only in the present age but also in the one to come." (Ephesians 1: 18–21)

☐ Omnipotence ☐ Omnipresence ☐ Omniscience ☐ Omnibenevolence

"For God so loved the world, that he gave his only Son, that whoever believes in him should not perish but have eternal life." (John 3:16)

☐ Omnipotence ☐ Omnipresence ☐ Omniscience ☐ Omnibenevolence

"And we pray this in order that you may live a life worthy of the Lord and may please him in every way: bearing fruit in every good work, growing in the knowledge of God, being strengthened with all power according to his glorious might so that you may have great endurance and patience, and joyfully giving thanks to the Father, who has qualified you to share in the inheritance of the saints in the kingdom of light." (Colossians 1:10–11)

☐ Omnipotence ☐ Omnipresence ☐ Omniscience ☐ Omnibenevolence

"But God shows His love for us in that while we were still sinners, Christ died for us." (Romans 5:8)

☐ Omnipotence ☐ Omnipresence ☐ Omniscience ☐ Omnibenevolence

"But God, being rich in mercy, because of the great love with which He loved us, even when weere dead in our trespasses, made us alive together with Christ - by grace you have been saved..." (Ephesians 2:4-5)

☐ Omnipotence ☐ Omnipresence ☐ Omniscience ☐ Omnibenevolence

"His divine power has given us everything we need for life and godliness through our knowledge of him who called us by his own glory and goodness." (2 Peter 1:3)

☐ Omnipotence ☐ Omnipresence ☐ Omniscience ☐ Omnibenevolence

"By wisdom the Lord laid the earth's foundations, by understanding he set the heavens in place; by his knowledge the deeps were divided, and the clouds let drop the dew." (Proverbs 3:19–20)

☐ Omnipotence ☐ Omnipresence ☐ Omniscience ☐ Omnibenevolence

"How many are your works, O Lord! In wisdom you made them all." (Psalm 104:24)

☐ Omnipotence ☐ Omnipresence ☐ Omniscience ☐ Omnibenevolence

"Surely you desire truth in the inner parts; you teach me wisdom in the inmost place." (Psalm 51:6)

☐ Omnipotence ☐ Omnipresence ☐ Omniscience ☐ Omnibenevolence

"No, in all these things we are more than conquerors through Him who loved us. For I am sure that neither death nor life, nor angels nor rulers, nor things present nor things to come, nor powers, nor height nor depth, nor anything else in all creation, will be able to separate us from the love of God in Christ Jesus our Lord." (Romans 8:37-39)

☐ Omnipotence ☐ Omnipresence ☐ Omniscience ☐ Omnibenevolence

"For God, who said, "Let light shine out of darkness." made his light shine in our hearts to give us the light of the knowledge of the glory of God in the face of Christ." (2 Corinthians 4:6)

☐ Omnipotence ☐ Omnipresence ☐ Omniscience ☐ Omnibenevolence

"He will be the sure foundation for your times, a rich store of salvation and wisdom and knowledge." (Isaiah 33:6)

☐ Omnipotence ☐ Omnipresence ☐ Omniscience ☐ Omnibenevolence

"Then Daniel praised the God of heaven and said: "Praise be to the name of God forever and ever; wisdom and power are his." (Daniel 2:19–20)

☐ Omnipotence ☐ Omnipresence ☐ Omniscience ☐ Omnibenevolence

"He changes times and seasons; he sets up kings and deposes them. He gives wisdom to the wise and knowledge to the discerning." (Daniel 2:21)

☐ Omnipotence ☐ Omnipresence ☐ Omniscience ☐ Omnibenevolence

""Oh, the depth of the riches of the wisdom and knowledge of God! How unsearchable his judgments, and his paths beyond tracing out!" (Romans 11:33)

☐ Omnipotence ☐ Omnipresence ☐ Omniscience ☐ Omnibenevolence

"In this the love of God was made manifest among us, that God sent His only Son into the world, so that we might live through Him. In this is love, not that we have loved God, but that He loved us and sent his Son to be the propitiation for our sins. Beloved, if God so loved us, we also ought to love one another." (1 John 2:4-5)

☐ Omnipotence ☐ Omnipresence ☐ Omniscience ☐ Omnibenevolence

"But the wisdom that comes from heaven is first of all pure; then peace-loving, considerate, submissive, full of mercy and good fruit, impartial and sincere." (James 3:17)

☐ Omnipotence ☐ Omnipresence ☐ Omniscience ☐ Omnibenevolence

"O Lord, you have searched me and you know me. You know when I sit and when I rise; you perceive my thoughts from afar. You discern my going out and my lying down; you are familiar with all my ways. Before a word is on my tongue you know it completely, O Lord." (Psalm 139: 1–4)

☐ Omnipotence ☐ Omnipresence ☐ Omniscience ☐ Omnibenevolence

"For this reason, since the day we heard about you, we have not stopped praying for you and asking God to fill you with the knowledge of his will through all spiritual wisdom and understanding." (Colossians 1:9)

☐ Omnipotence   ☐ Omnipresence   ☐ Omniscience   ☐ Omnibenevolence

"My purpose is that they may be encouraged in heart and united in love, so that they may have the full riches of complete understanding, in order that they may know the mystery of God, namely, Christ, in whom are hidden all the treasures of wisdom and knowledge." (Colossians 2:2–3)

☐ Omnipotence   ☐ Omnipresence   ☐ Omniscience   ☐ Omnibenevolence

Whoever does not love does not know God because God is love. (1 John 4:8)

☐ Omnipotence   ☐ Omnipresence   ☐ Omniscience   ☐ Omnibenevolence

"Where can I go from your Spirit? Where can I flee from your presence? If I go up to the heavens, you are there; if I make my bed in the depths, you are there. If I rise on the wings of the dawn, if I settle on the far side of the sea, even there your hand will guide me, your right hand will hold me fast. If I say, "Surely the darkness will hide me and the light become night around me," even the darkness will not be dark to you; the night will shine like the day, for darkness is as light to you. For you created my inmost being; you knit me together in my mother's womb. I praise you because I am fearfully and wonderfully made; your works are wonderful, I know that full well. My frame was not hidden from you when I was made in the secret place. When I was woven together in the depths of the earth, your eyes saw my unformed body. All the days ordained for me were written in your book before one of them came to be. How precious to me are your thoughts, O God! How vast is the sum of them! Were I to count them, they would outnumber the grains of sand. When I awake, I am still with you." (Psalm 139: 8–18)

☐ Omnipotence   ☐ Omnipresence   ☐ Omniscience   ☐ Omnibenevolence

"Finally, be strong in the Lord and in his mighty power." (Ephesians 6:10)

☐ Omnipotence   ☐ Omnipresence   ☐ Omniscience   ☐ Omnibenevolence

The message that we should received from this portion of our study is that God's power has no limits, for He is powerful enough to do anything. His presence has no boundaries, which makes everything visible to Him and provides the ability for Him to dwell in each of us fully and simultaneously. His knowledge has no end, for everything possible is known to Him. And His love has no measure, for He is infinitely perfect in all things.

Because life presents many crossroads at points in our lives where we have to make many decisions, let's focus on God's omniscience a little more closely, particularly as it relates to His illuminating wisdom.

According to James 3:17, how is God's wisdom described?

_____

_____

Why do you think it is described this way?

_____

According to James 1:5, how should you obtain wisdom that will light your path?

_____

_____

Proverbs 2:6 confirms that wisdom is given by God. From where, specifically, does it say wisdom comes?

_____

What else does Proverbs 2:7–9 say God will do for us?

_____

According to Ecclesiastes 2:26, to whom does God give wisdom, knowledge, and happiness, and what does He give the sinner?

_____

_____

What does 2 Peter 1:2 say we will receive in abundance through the knowledge of God and of Jesus?

_____

_____

<u>Being God's</u> LightWe not only need to receive God's light in order to have spiritual growth that will lead to abundant fruitfulness...we also need to be the light.

What does Jesus call us in Matthew 5:13? _____

What does He command us to do? _____

Why is this important to God? _____

How does Matthew 6:22 say your light can be visible?

_____

_____

According to 2 Corinthians: 4–6, God made his light shine in our hearts to give us the light of the knowledge of the glory of the God in the face of Christ. Why does the verse say some are blinded to this light?

_____

_____

What are some 'gods' that exist today that are doing the same thing?

_____

_____

_____

_____

Who, according to 2 Corinthians 11:14, masquerades as an angel of light, hoping to distract humans from God's light? _____

Yes, Satan will try to distract us from everything of God, including and especially His light. The next chapter will discuss how we can best be on guard against him and those who work with him to deter us from Christ and he plans He has for growth in our fruitful garden.

Reflection

According to John 1:5, God is light. Review the definitions and scriptures above and think of some ways that you would like God's light to be present in your life. Write your answers below.

_____

_____

_____

_____

_____

_____

_____

_____

_____

_____

_____

_____

_____

_____

_____

_____

_____

Relatable Bible Figure

- Solomon

Solomon was one of the wisest rulers to have ever lived. With the exception of Jesus, of course, many consider him to be the wisest man who ever lived, filled with the light of wisdom that only God can provide.

It's interesting to note that Solomon was conceived during the time of grief for David as he had recently lost a child after pleading with God to save his son. Why did God not save David's son?

In this case, it was because of sin and because He would later use sufferings in David's life as a testament to His own glory. Despite the many sins that David would commit in his life, God continued to bless him out of faithfulness. Solomon appears to be one such great blessing.

According to 2 Samuel 2:24, how did God feel about Solomon at the time of his birth?

_____

God knew Solomon and knew already that he would both do great things and shameful things throughout his life, but despite anything he could do wrong, God knew what he could do right and loved him for that. God responds the same way today. God knows that we will do many things wrong, but His focus on us is what we will do right and it is these things that bring Him such delight in us. For that reason, He also blesses us with light despite our wretched lives.

How did Solomon receive his great blessings? According to 2 Chronicles, Solomon, who was the third king of Israel and David's chosen heir, sought wisdom early in his life.

How does 2 Chronicles 1:1-10 say he obtained his great wisdom?

_____

In 2 Chronicles 1: 11-12, how did God reply to Solomon's request?

_____

_____

Evidence of Solomon's great wisdom can be seen in the Proverbs which in contrast to the poetic nature of the Psalms, are simply simple instructions to teach people how they should morally and spiritually conduct themselves in their daily lives. Most people simply refer to them as "wise sayings", but they are much more than that. Because they were inspired by God, they reflect the personal thoughts and direction of God himself. And just as the Psalms still retain their relevance for today, so do the Proverbs. Here's an example of one such Proverb for your reference and readiness as we begin our journey towards the next chapter which discusses destructive forces:

Proverbs 20

1   *Wine is a mocker and beer a brawler; whoever is led astray by them is not wise.*
2   *A king's wrath is like the roar of a lion; he who angers him forfeits his life.*
3   *It is to a man's honor to avoid strife, but every fool is quick to quarrel.*
4   *A sluggard does not plow in season; so at harvest time he looks but finds nothing.*

5   *The purposes of a man's heart are deep waters,*
    but a man of understanding draws them out.

6   *Many a man claims to have unfailing love, but*
    a faithful man who can find?

7   *The righteous man leads a blameless life;*
    blessed are his children after him.

8   *When a king sits on his throne to judge, he*
    winnows out all evil with his eyes.

9   *Who can say, "I have kept my heart pure; I am*
    clean and without sin"?

10 *Differing weights and differing measures— the*
    Lord detests them both.

11 *Even a child is known by his actions, by whether*
    his conduct is pure and right.

12 *Ears that hear and eyes that see— the LORD*
    has made them both.

13 *Do not love sleep or you will grow poor; stay*
    awake and you will have food to spare.

14 *"It's no good, it's no good!" says the buyer; then*
    off he goes and boasts about his purchase.

15 *Gold there is, and rubies in abundance, but*
    lips that speak knowledge are a rare jewel.

16 *Take the garment of one who puts up security*
    for a stranger; hold it in pledge if he does it for
    a wayward woman.

17 *Food gained by fraud tastes sweet to a man, but*
    he ends up with a mouth full of gravel.

18 *Make plans by seeking advice; if you wage war,*
    obtain guidance.

19 *A gossip betrays a confidence; so avoid a man*
    who talks too much.

20 *If a man curses his father or mother, his lamp*
    will be snuffed out in pitch darkness.

21 *An inheritance quickly gained at the beginning*
    will not be blessed at the end.

22 *Do not say, "I'll pay you back for this wrong!"*
    Wait for the Lord, and He will deliver you.

23 *The Lord detests differing weights, and*
    dishonest scales do not please him.

24 *A man's steps are directed by the LORD. How*
    then can anyone understand his own way?

25 *It is a trap for a man to dedicate something*
    rashly and only later to consider his vows.

26   *A wise king winnows out the wicked; he drives the threshing wheel over them.*

27   *The lamp of the Lord searches the spirit of a man; it searches out his inmost being.*

28   *Love and faithfulness keep a king safe; through love his throne is made secure.*

29   *The glory of young men is their strength, gray hair the splendor of the old.*

30   *Blows and wounds cleanse away evil, and beatings purge the inmost being.*

Unfortunately, Solomon had a weakness for foreign women and, as a result, had many wives which both negatively influenced his leadership and his loyalty to God. But it was in his weakness and seeking the Lord's help, that he was able to write the Proverbs with such credibility. Had he always remained true to his calling as a leader, he would likely have missed some experiences that helped him to grow spiritually. No doubt you have had similar experiences. I know I have. In many ways, my mistakes in life have pulled me closer to God and because of His forgiveness, I know that my mistakes will be used for good and I have certainly grown spiritually as a result of the light that God has provided through my errors in judgment.

Solomon is included in the list of relational bible figures because he not only received the light of God in wisdom, but because God loved him and blessed him in spite of his weaknesses and sins. This is important for you to know especially if you are doubting whether you are worthy of God's light. None of us are worthy of it, but because of His love and mercy, we receive God's light as a testament to His faithfulness. Just as God was faithful to Solomon, He will be faithful to you in your pursuit of the light that will lead you on your journey to abundance with Him.

Blessed Assurances

- God will illuminate or make visible, the answers to the tough questions you might about life through His Word.
- God will light your path and lead you exactly where He knows you need to be if you seek Him.
- God has a distinct plan and pre-destined purpose for your life.
- God wants to lead you to your pursuit of fruitfulness because it brings Him glory.
- You are worthy of receiving God's light despite a past that might not have been so clean because Christ made you worthy to be part of His adopted family based on your belief in Him.

Fertilize Yourself This Week

Allow the unfolding of God's Word to give you light. This week, make time to read the Bible a little each day as you seek the illumination from God in response to the questions that you have about your current path and in the list you made during your "reflection" time. You can read from any section of the Bible, but the Psalms may be especially beneficial.

As you read, also spend some quiet time asking God to provide his illuminating light to you in all areas of your life. To help you get started, here is a similar prayer from David for your reference.

"Show me your ways, O Lord, teach me your paths; guide me in your truth and teach me, for you are God my Savior, and my hope is in you all day long. Remember, O LORD, your great mercy and love, for they are from of old." (Psalm 25: 4–6)

Chapter Five: Destructive Forces

Outline

I. Types of Destructive Forces
    A. Weeds
    B. Pests
II. Protection Against Destructive Forces
    A. Weed barrier (below the surface to keep weeds from forming)
    B. Mulch (On the surface and surrounding the plant to keep weeds from penetrating)
    C. Fertilizer
    D. Repellant

Foundation Scriptures

> *"The field is the world, and the good seed stands for the sons of the kingdom. The weeds are the sons of the evil one, and the enemy who sows them is the devil."*
> *(Matthew 13:38)*

Introduction

Our foundation scripture for this week comes from a parable of weeds that Jesus told. It conveniently falls in the same chapter as the parable of seeds that we studied previously. If you recall, the parable of seeds discusses the conditions necessary for the seed to grow to abundant fruition. The parable in our foundation scripture for this chapter, however, brings into discussion the weeds that also have a tendency to grow. As with all parables that Jesus told, underneath the basic story was a spiritual message. In this parable, Jesus compares followers of Christ to good seeds and those who live to follow their sinful nature as weeds. Of course, Satan is the one who plants the seed that encourages others to sin.

It is important to remember that because we are human, even the most devout Christians sin. It's in our nature, just as it is in Satan's nature to sow the seeds of sin. Satan not only wants to sow the seeds; he also wants to see them grow roots and multiply. He not only wants it, He *delights* in it. He is fully aware of all of the laws of nature and knows that he can successfully choke out the fruitful presence of God if he is successful in his endeavor to grow sin. He delights in having many different varieties of seeds that he can plant at any given time and especially loves to plant discord, jealousy, fear, and resentment because these seeds often go unnoticed until deep roots have formed. So be warned, stay alert, and maintain watchfulness over your garden. The day when the enemy will certainly try to attack is here.

For our study in this chapter, we will dig deeper into our knowledge about Satan's threats to our inner garden of tranquil peace and take an in-depth look at how we can protect ourselves against him.

Definitions

Natural Weed

-noun

1. a valueless plant growing wild, especially one that grows on cultivated ground to the exclusion or injury of the desired crop.
2. any undesirable or troublesome plant, especially one that grows profusely where it is not wanted: *The vacant lot was covered with weeds.*

To Naturally Weed

-verb

1. to free from weeds or troublesome plants; root out weeds from: *to weed a garden.*
2. to root out or remove (a weed or weeds), as from a garden (often followed by *out*): *to weed out crab grass from a lawn.*
3. to remove as being undesirable, inefficient, or superfluous (often followed by *out*): *to weed out inexperienced players.*
4. to rid (something) of undesirable or superfluous elements.
Source: Unabridged Random House Dictionary

Spiritual Weed

-noun

1. a valueless substance that grows in your life, especially one that grows on a cultivated Christian foundation for the prevention of the desired fruitfulness.
2. any undesirable or troublesome attribute, especially one that grows profusely where God does not want it.

To Spiritually Weed

-verb

1. to free from sin or troublesome attributes
2. to root or remove (a weed or weeds), as from your life
3. to remove anything as being undesirable or ineffective

Natural Pest

-noun

1. an annoying or troublesome person, animal, or thing; nuisance
2. an insect or other small animal that harms or destroys garden plants, trees, et cetera
3. a deadly epidemic disease, especially a plague; pestilence.

Spiritual Pest

-noun

1. a troublesome or wicked person who distracts you from God.
2. a person who harms or destroys your spiritual growth by invading your soil with a negative influence and growing roots of discord.
3. a spiritually deadly epidemic of society caused by Satan as a vector of spiritual pestilence.

Scripture Study: Defending with the Word

Types of Destructive Forces

• Weeds

As defined above, a weed is an undesirable substance that grows in our life and threatens to choke out our spiritual growth. Unfortunately, we don't always see the substance as undesirable even though God does. Very often, weeds can be very deceiving as they don't appear to be sin.

Think about the appearance of a dandelion or a thistle. Both have the beauty and appearance of a flower, yet both are weeds. Just like a child who can't tell the difference and brings their mother a bouquet of dandelion weeds, we can be guilty of doing the same with our Heavenly Father. We tend to forget that it's Satan's cunning nature to slip a few unnoticed seeds in our soil, seeds that seem so harmless when they start to sprout. So harmless, in fact, that we almost welcome those plants into our garden because they appear green and floral.

That's where danger enters as a wolf in a sheep's skin. Once a sinful seed penetrates the soil, it's impossible to be filled to the measure with the fullness of Christ. If unnoticed or unattended, the sinful seed ultimately can germinate and then take root where it will limit or even prevent fruit-bearing. Common roots that form this way are roots of bitterness, anger, fear, and insecurity.

According to 1 Timothy 6:10, what is another negative root? Why is it so bad?

_____

_____

And that's how all weeds are to varying degrees. Anything that causes us to wander from our path of faith should be considered a weed. To make sure that we are on alert for these subtle seeds, we should ask ourselves if a sprout in our lives glorifies God in any way. If you aren't sure about the answer or know that it is a definite *no*, then you are dealing with a weed and need to take the necessary steps to remove it from your garden as described later in this chapter.

Keep in mind, however, that once a seed has germinated and formed deep roots, it will begin to multiply, and then it will be virtually impossible for you to remove it on your own. Instead, you must completely remove your hands from the weeds and allow God to pull them up by the roots.

According to Matthew 15:13, what specifically will God pull up by the roots?

_____

Only then will your original plant flourish and subsequently bear fruit.

What types of behaviors can have such devastating effects on your spiritual growth?

Read the following scriptures and identify the weeds below.

Proverbs 28:25 _____

1 John 2:15 _____

1 John 2:16 _____

Titus 2:12 _____

1 Corinthians 3:3 _____

Galatians 5:26 _____

Philippians 2:3 _____

Galatians 5:19–21 _____

Romans 1:29–30 _____

James 2:1 _____

Romans 13:2 _____

Ephesians 6:4 _____

Matthew 7:1 _____

Proverbs 12:22 _____

Where do these weeds really start?

We all know that the weeds do not come from God. Let's take a look at a couple of scriptures that clarify and/or confirm this for us.

Where does Mark 7:21–23 say specific weeds come from?

_____

_____

Who is responsible for the weeds according to Matthew 13:38-39?

_____

_____

Later in this chapter, we will discuss effective ways to destroy the weeds, but for now, let's first take a look at another threat to our spiritual growth that we must also address.

- Pests

As noted above, a pest is a person or being that distracts us from our focus on God. We recognize that these are the people who are negative influences and continually attempt to devour our energy, our focus, our time, and our other resources. They ultimately prevent healthy fruit from being produced.

While it may seem odd to use this particular noun in a Bible study for life application, it is actually biblically based. The Greek word "loimos" as used in the New Testament is defined as "a pestilent fellow, a pest" and can be found in Acts 24:5 where the NIV version renders it "troublemaker".

For this study, we will focus on three main types of pests that that can affect our spiritual growth.

In the first group of pests are the **predators.** By definition, a predator is one who preys on others. These are generally nonbelievers who choose a lifestyle inconsistent with biblical values and are always on the lookout for anyone else to join in on their earthly endeavors. This group includes those who are sexually immoral, drunkards, thieves … and any other type of person who wants others to join in on their perceived fun. Unfortunately, more often than you might think, a

Christian may give in and succumb to the pressure because the pest makes it seem so appealing. But even just one night of passion or partying can have devastating effects on spiritual growth.

The **pathogens** make up the next group. These are the ones who have a virus-like nature that spreads negativity to others very quickly. They are the people who spread contagious seeds of discord wherever they go. They tend to be sly and blend well in society, yet use deceit, lies, and gossip in addition to the other negative behaviors they sow, either consciously or unconsciously, to affect the lives of others. As a result, they tend to try to pull us down rather than lifting us up. Unfortunately, this group can and does often include Christians.

Last are the **parasites**. This group of pests includes those who receive support or advantages from us but fail to provide any useful or proper return. Parasites often attach themselves to others to receive spiritual and emotional nourishment rather than attaching to and seeking to be filled only God. As a result, they frequently steal our time and energy, leaving us little time or energy to focus on God. Again, it is an unfortunate fact that many of these individuals are also Christians. I want to be clear that I'm not implying imply that anyone who seeks our hospitality or help is a pest or parasite. That certainly is not the case; we are encouraged to be hospitable and help others! A pest or parasite, however, uses an excessive amount of our resources and because their clinging to us is not directed by God, it robs us of time spent for and with Him.

It is important for you to be aware of the various types of pests to help you identify their presence in your life, but for the purposes of eliminating the pests or their influence on you, we will look at them as a whole.

Before we go there, however, I want to separate from the general group of pests those who are Christians. It is possible for a Christian to have pestilent tendencies with whom God will deal as described below, but it's also possible—and all of us have done it—to sin against another unintentionally. I point this out because I don't want you to end this lesson thinking that you should distance yourself from Christians who wrong you. That certainly isn't what the Bible directs us to do. Sin and wrongdoings are unfortunately in our human nature and need to be accounted for and dealt with appropriately for the ultimate glory of God. Simply turning your back on someone who sinned against you would fail to make that happen.

Instead, how does Matthew 18:15 say we should respond when a Christian sins against us?

_____

In our human relationships, we tend to turn away from others in hatred or resentment, often engaging in gossip against the one who hurt us, but that is not what God commanded. We are told instead to go to that person first, as difficult as it may be for us. We should then forgive the person. And not only should we forgive them personally, but we should make sure that we forgive them deep within our hearts no matter how many times we are sinned against. *According to Matthew 18: 21–22, how many times should we forgive someone?*

_____

In doing so, we immediately remove any seeds of bitterness or anger towards that person and eliminate all chances of having destructive roots form in our lives.

In contrast, however, there are those planted in the world by Satan. The Bible makes it clear that Matthew 18:15 refers to *brothers in Christ*. Timothy, on the other hand, discusses the presence of non-Christian pests. In 2 Timothy 3:3–7, Paul describes pests who are "lovers of themselves, lovers of money, boastful, proud, abusive, disobedient to their parents, ungrateful, unholy, without love, unforgiving, slanderous, without self-control, brutal, not lovers of the good, treacherous, rash, conceited, lovers of pleasure rather than lovers of God … the kind who worm their way into homes and gain control over weak-willed women, who are loaded down with sins and are swayed by all kinds of evil desires."

What does Timothy instruct us to do with such pests?

Likewise, Matthew tells us to have nothing to do with false prophets, or the ones who appear to come in the Lord's name, but actually come on behalf of Satan. How does Matthew 7:15 describe them?

I want to post a warning to you here that there are some people who profess to be Christians and even proclaim the name of Jesus Christ, but have not truly been saved. Just as you can't adopt a child without the official approval of the court, you can't be adopted into the kingdom of Heaven without the approval of God. A child can certainly proclaim someone to be his parent, but unless there has been an official decree, that child is not the person's son or daughter. In order to be adopted into God's family, we must first provide a profession of our faith and proclaim him as our Lord and Savior. We must also be born again. This means that we are dead to our former sinful selves and are reborn as ones who follow a path without sin. This doesn't mean that once you are a Christian, you never sin, but it does mean that you don't actively follow a sinful path. Some people, however, take on the name of Christ and may even show up in church each week, but are never truly born again and thus are not truly Christians.

How does Matthew 7:16–20 say we will be able to know these people are weeds?

The Bible makes it clear that pests, particularly those who are false prophets, are a problem. One of the main reasons is because not all Christians have matured. Some are still tender, young sprouts who can be swayed by teachings that are not of God, but appear to be Biblical. Satan has a crafty way of twisting the truth to make us think we might be following God when we are actually traveling away from God. In fact, there are many modern religions that encourage believers to praise God and love one another, but entirely leave out the role and existence of Jesus Christ (and, if asked, would deny Him). Yet their teachings sound good and feel good, so many believers follow these teachings not fully considering that without Christ, it's impossible to be a *Christ*ian!

Read 2 Peter 2, which describes the path of the false teachers. What does this chapter say will happen to them because of what they do to us?

_____

How else does the Word say God has and will punish the wicked?

Read the following scriptures and document the methods.

Psalm 107: 33–34 _____

Psalm 58:9 _____

Psalm11:6 _____

1 Samuel 2:8–10 _____

What does Deuteronomy 28:38 describe as the outcome of your life if you follow a sinful path?

_____

Read Proverbs 16:4–6. What three concepts do these verses reinforce from our current and previous study together? What do you think the author meant when He wrote "through the fear of the Lord a man avoids evil"?

_____

_____

_____

Protection from Destructive Forces

- God as a weed barrier

Have you ever planted a garden? If so, did you use a weed barrier? If you are unfamiliar with a weed barrier, it is a plastic or cloth-like material that is laid at the bottom of your empty flower or vegetable garden before the pure soil is placed in the bed. By having an impermeable foundation, it's virtually impossible for weeds to emerge from the impure soil below the barrier. For us, God is our weed barrier. He is a solid foundation that prevents weeds and pests from destroying our growth if we allow him to be an impermeable part in our lives.

What specific promise does God offer to reinforce his role as weed barrier in Malachi 3:11?

_____

_____

There are many ways that God prevents forces from devouring our crops. One such way is through the use of His Word. Let's look at some specific ways God's instruction can save us from the deadly destruction of weeds that threaten to choke out our spiritual growth.

In Chapter Two, during our study of the parable of the seed, we learned about the seed that fell among the thorns grew up and choked the plants. Revisit Luke 8:14 to identify again the meaning of this part of the parable. Write your answer below.

_____

_____

_____

In contrast, how does Luke 8:15 say to ensure a bountiful crop?

_____

_____

What specific instruction does Romans 12:2 give us for us to retain?

_____

_____

Avoiding conformity to the pattern of the world is sometimes easier said than done. Humans in today's society tend to get easily distracted by worldly things, especially worldly pleasures, without even realizing that they are sinning and ultimately wandering from God. But just because we *accidently* do it doesn't make it acceptable. The truth is that you can neither live your life for the world and be distracted by God nor live your life for God and be distracted by the world. You must simply live your life for God.

So in trying to live our lives for God, we are often on a path wondering which way will get us to where we want to be. But how do we know which way to go?

The book of Matthew offers insight into the contrast between following a path of sin and a path that leads to life spent in fertile soil. How is this described in Matthew 7:13, and which way should you go?

_____

_____

_____

But how do you know which is the narrow gate? I'm sure, after the last chapter, that you have a pretty good idea. However, read Proverbs 4 and underline all the instructions contained within the Word.

Proverbs 4

1 *"Listen, my sons, to a father's instruction; pay attention and gain understanding.*

2 *I give you sound learning, so do not forsake my teaching.*

3 *When I was a boy in my father's house, still tender, and an only child of my mother,*

4 *he taught me and said, "Lay hold of my words with all your heart; keep my commands and you will live.*

5 *"Get wisdom, get understanding; do not forget my words or swerve from them.*

6 *"Do not forsake wisdom, and she will protect you; love her, and she will watch over you.*

7 *"Wisdom is supreme; therefore get wisdom. Though it cost all you have, get understanding.*

8 *" Esteem her, and she will exalt you; embrace her, and she will honor you.*

9 *"She will set a garland of grace on your head and present you with a crown of splendor.*

10 *"Listen, my son, accept what I say, and the years of your life will be many.*

11 *"I guide you in the way of wisdom and lead you along straight paths.*

12 *"When you walk, your steps will not be hampered; when you run, you will not stumble.*

13 *"Hold on to instruction, do not let it go; guard it well, for it is your life.*

14 *"Do not set foot on the path of the wicked or walk in the way of evil men.*

15 *"Avoid it, do not travel on it; turn from it and go on your way.*

16 *"For they cannot sleep till they do evil; they are robbed of slumber till they make someone fall.*

17 *"They eat the bread of wickedness and drink the wine of violence.*

18 *"The path of the righteous is like the first gleam of dawn, shining ever brighter till the full light of day.*

19 *"But the way of the wicked is like deep darkness; they do not know what makes them stumble.*

20 *"My son, pay attention to what I say; listen closely to my words.*

21 *"Do not let them out of your sight, keep them within your heart;*

22 *for they are life to those who find them and health to a man's whole body.*

23 *"Above all else, guard your heart, for it is the wellspring of life.*

24 *"Put away perversity from your mouth; keep corrupt talk far from your lips.*

25 *"Let your eyes look straight ahead, fix your gaze directly before you.*

26 *"Make level paths for your feet and take only ways that are firm.*

27 *"Do not swerve to the right or the left; keep your foot from evil."*

Isn't it wonderful that God provides us with such clear instructions as the above passages contain? Remember, any time you need instruction on anything in life, turn to the Word and you will find explicit detail, just as in the above Psalm, that will tell you specifically how to live your life.

The Bible offers many wise instructions and can certainly teach us how to avoid evil ones who might divert you from the path you walk with God, yet there are times when pests just seem to appear out of nowhere, trying to tempt you to leave the safe, bright path of the Lord.

What does Psalm 37:7 say you should do when this happens?

_____

_____

Fortunately, being still before the Lord is much easier when we find that we don't have to fight against the wicked, but can simply rely on God to be our assurance and protection. Reliance on God is a theme in many scriptures that describe God as a protective barrier, the concept that we are discussing in this chapter.

Read the following scriptures that relate to God as a physical barrier.

Genesis 15:1	*2 Samuel 22:31*	*Psalm 3:3*	*Psalm 5:12*
Psalm 18:30	*Psalm 18:35*	*Psalm 28:7*	*Psalm 33:20*
Psalm 84:11	*Psalm 119:114*	*Proverbs 30:5*	

Leah Vintila

What do they have in common?

What does this figurative usage mean to you?

What does the author of Psalm 84 say of his preference to God as his shield and why?

Although the author is unknown, we do know that the writer of Psalm 91 had a close, personal relationship with God and had almost certainly experienced the comforting shelter of God as God confronted the same pests that we've studied in this chapter. Read this Psalm carefully and then document below the reassurance it gives you.

Psalm 91

1. *"He who dwells in the shelter of the Most High will rest in the shadow of the Almighty.*
2. *I will say of the lord, "He is my refuge and my fortress, my God, in whom I trust."*
3. *Surely he will save you from the fowler's snare and from the deadly pestilence.*
4. *He will cover you with his feathers, and under his wings you will find refuge; his faithfulness will be your shield and rampart.*
5. *You will not fear the terror of night, nor the arrow that flies by day,*
6. *nor the pestilence that stalks in the darkness, nor the plague that destroys at midday.*
7. *A thousand may fall at your side, ten thousand at your right hand, but it will not come near you.*
8. *You will only observe with your eyes and see the punishment of the wicked.*
9. *If you make the Most High your dwelling— even the lord, who is my refuge—*

10   *then no harm will befall you, no disaster will come near your tent.*

11   *For he will command his angels concerning you to guard you in all your ways;*

12   *they will lift you up in their hands, so that you will not strike your foot against a stone.*

13   *You will tread upon the lion and the cobra; you will trample the great lion and the serpent.*

14   *"Because he loves me," says the lord, "I will rescue him; I will protect him, for he acknowledges my name.*

15   *"He will call upon me, and I will answer him; I will be with him in trouble, I will deliver him and honor him.*

16   *"With long life will I satisfy him and show him my salvation."*

Personal Reassurances:

_____

_____

_____

_____

- Mulch

In addition to providing prevention in the form of the inner barrier, God also allows us to have exterior protection.

If you were to look up the function of mulch in horticulture, here's what you would find:

- It helps conserve water in the soil.

- It keeps weed growth down.

- It helps to keep the roots cooler than the air above the ground.

- It protects trees from damage from mowers and trimmers.

- It helps to prevent erosion.

- It improves the appearance of your landscaping.

Christians function in the same manner as mulch through fellowship. Through our Christian fellowship, we insulate other believers against the outside world. Unlike the pests around us, who pull us down, Christians who are positive influences uplift us. The Christians we associate with will assist in filling us with living water when they allow themselves to be used by Christ to help us remember and retain His words in our life through their counsel. Those we keep fellowship with will also keep our weed growth down because their fellowship crowds out pests. If we allow other Christians to surround us, they will help keep our roots cool by limiting the heated situations that we encounter or providing accountability to help us when we do. They will certainly provide a barrier against the cold outside world that seems so abrasive to us at times. Christian friends will also help prevent erosion in the same manner by providing that outer barrier to strengthen us. And finally, would you agree that having the right influences in our lives improves our appearance? Yes, it does. It affects our demeanor, the expression and attitude we show the world, and therefore improves the general impression that others have of us. As the old saying goes, "You are who you associate with," and that can be a very telling statement to just about anyone.

What does 1 Thessalonians 5:11 instruct us to do?

_____

In Romans1:11–12, what does Paul say we should use to help each other?

_____

In addition to encouraging one another, what additional instructions does Hebrews 10:25 provide?

_____

According to Matthew 18:20, what is the benefit of coming together?

_____

As we can see, the Bible offers much encouragement for believers to come together in love and support for mutual encouragement. It's important to consider, however, that the enemy will try his hardest to keep us away from this type of fellowship. He will use many things including some of the things we find in non-fertile soil, such as insecurities or distractions, to keep us from joining in groups of Christians. It's up to each of us to encourage others to join in this fellowship, especially those who may be timid or even those who profess they are too busy to have time for it. We also have to each take the ownership upon ourselves to take part. Perhaps you are the one who is uncomfortable taking part in fellowship or the one perceiving that you are too busy. If either of these define you, then realize that the very nature of it being listed several times in the bible as a command makes it something that you should assure that you do. If you are insecure, press against those insecurities, giving your fears to God, and engage in fellowship anyway. If you are too busy, then take some time to reevaluate your schedule and prioritize time for this. I've personally lived both ends of this spectrum and have been too insecure at times or too busy at others and can testify to the difference it can make when the decision is made to fellowship anyway. I really don't think you can get much more shy than I once was and yet, today I thrive on the blessing that God gives me through the Christian fellowship and intimate relationships I enjoy each day! He wants to bless each of you with the same.

• Fertilizer

By definition, fertilizers are compounds given to plants to promote growth. God uses humans in much the same way. How does He do this? He does so by creating the fertilizer from the compost that has occurred in the lives of His people.

Do you know someone who has experienced a terrible tragedy and then turned the situation around to help others? Most of us do. In fact, the strongest organizers of many worthwhile organizations such as MADD (Mothers Against Drunk Drivers) started their journey with an unfathomably horrible life event. Most people, fortunately, don't have that kind of experience to share with others, but most people do have experiences that can be made into fertilizer. Any experience in which one receives mercy, comfort, and/or salvation from God qualifies as a fertilizer-building experience. One person may not experience quite the level of tragedy as another, but still go through a fierce storm and emerge from that storm a strong survivor who is later able to help others in the same situation.

Most people are probably not consciously seeking opportunities to be fertilizer immediately after the storm, but God makes certain we are well-equipped to use our survivor skills to help others do the same. For me, it was the infertility, but it would be several years before my use as fertilizer was fully called upon. God has also used the death of close loved ones for the same purpose. For you it could be similar things or something completely different; only time will tell how God chooses to use you.

The important point is that God has a purpose. He purposefully creates fertilizer out of our not-so-pleasant pasts and purposefully puts that fertilizer to good use in the lives of others. Fertilization from others during hard seasons of our life help us to keep hope and faith alive against whatever we are facing. It helps us to stand firm against our adversaries (pests) and it should help to eliminate the negative thoughts (weeds) that want to penetrate our minds. As a result, it comforts us.

Who does 2 Corinthians 1:3 say provides comfort to us and how does it say that comfort is used?

_____

_____

Yes, He provides comfort so that we can later provide that same comfort to others. It's important to remember that although God uses others in this role, they (and later we) are simply tools for Him. It is only His working through people that provides for the intended comfort, hope and faith.

- Repellant

What does 1 Peter 5 say the enemy does?

_____

As Christians, we face many attacks from the enemy. No doubt, we all have experienced these, likely in increasing number when we have attempted to grow closer to God as we are doing through this study. Yes, he is prowling around seeking someone to devour. And we are often easy targets. It's in our nature to be easily distracted by the world around us and with self...especially when we are created as emotional beings. The enemy often leverages our own weaknesses to accomplish his work. And through our own weaknesses that are already familiar ground to us, he can move with much more stealth and successfully remove our focus just enough to sow weeds while we aren't looking. Satan knows full well that even a few seeds of discord, bitterness, anger, insecurity, or any other negative substance can grow quickly to choke out all God's light from your presence. After all, what Satan wants more than anything is to limit the number of witnesses who praise God's name. All who praise are acting as fertilizer to themselves and others, and this divine agenda certainly doesn't mix well with the Devil's destructive agenda.

What four things does 1 Peter 5:6-9 instruct us to do?

_____

_____

_____

_____

In many translations of Peter 5:9, the word stand is used, noting that we are to stand firm in our faith. We are also instructed to stand in the book of Ephesians. Standing helps to assure that our focus is on God and reminds us that He will be the One to fight our battles for us. We are not lying in slumber, nor are we moving forward in our own weak abilities. We are simply standing and letting Him take the greater action in our lives as we stand firm.

Read the following and underline all the instructions this verse provides.

Ephesians 6:10–18

"Finally, be strong in the Lord and in his mighty power. Put on the full armor of God so that you can take your stand against the devil's schemes. For our struggle is not against flesh and blood, but against the rulers, against the authorities, against the powers of this dark world and against the spiritual forces of evil in the heavenly realms. Therefore put on the full armor of God, so that when the day of evil comes, you may be able to stand your ground, and after you have done everything, to stand. Stand firm then, with the belt of truth buckled around your waist, with the

breastplate of righteousness in place, and with your feet fitted with the readiness that comes from the gospel of peace. In addition to all this, take up the shield of faith, with which you can extinguish all the flaming arrows of the evil one. Take the helmet of salvation and the sword of the Spirit, which is the word of God. And pray in the Spirit on all occasions with all kinds of prayers and requests. With this in mind, be alert and always keep on praying for all the saints."

Ephesians 6:10–18 is a very powerful scripture. Let's study it closely to help grasp the full meaning of its intent.

First, we have the belt of truth. As previously noted, Satan wants to make us doubt God, and the best way he can do this is through lies. Just as he cunningly lied to Eve, he will lie to you so cunningly that his lie can sound like the truth. By wearing the belt of real truth from God, you can readily deflect and defeat Satan's lies.

Next, we receive the breastplate of righteousness. Notice where the breastplate is worn—directly over the heart. Because our heart contains our love, trust, and other deep emotions, Satan will certainly try to attack our hearts. Remember, as Mark said in Chapter 7, weeds form in the heart, so that's a favored spot for Satan to sprinkle some seeds. But we belong to God and not to this world, so God gives us the breastplate of righteousness because, through righteousness, we are identified as belonging to Him. Because God loves us, He gives us this breastplate to protect our hearts against Satan's attacks.

The third piece of armor we are given is the footgear of readiness. What must we be ready for? We must be prepared to spread the good news about God. Satan wants us to think that telling others about the good news of Christ is a worthless and hopeless task, or that the size of task is too big for us. Satan encourages us to think that the task would be better suited for people greater than us. But the footgear of readiness provides for our readiness to tell others about the saving grace of the Lord. This is a significant piece of armor because many people fear sharing the gospel. We can be assured because of this verse that we are equipped for this task by God and not of our own ability. And while God does call some people to evangelize for Him with the gospel news as its own message, for most people this piece of armor simply reflects our testimony and how the good news is found in our story. It is most often our testimony which tells the greatness of His love, grace, and mercy that is good news to people.

Following our footgear, God gives us a shield of faith, specifically noting that we can use it to extinguish Satan's flaming arrows. What types of arrows does aim he at us? Arrows of temptation, insults, and stumbling blocks that threaten to damage our spiritual growth permanently if we allow them to penetrate us.

Next, we receive the helmet of salvation. As previously mentioned, Satan wants us to doubt God and His abilities to perform wonders. Because our knowledge of the Lord and His abilities originates in our minds, a helmet protects the knowledge there—the truths we know about the God who saves us.

Finally, we receive the sword of the Spirit, which is the Word of God. It's interesting to notice that the sword is the only weapon of offense in this list of armor. There are certainly times when we need to fight against Satan and not just protect ourselves from him. Whenever we sense that Satan's attack is near, we need to trust in the truth of God's Word and rely on it to be our offensive against evil.

How do we assure that we are always wearing our armor? As we studied earlier in Ephesians 6:18, we are to pray in the spirit on all occasions with all kinds of prayers and requests. We need to be in continual communion, or intimate communication, with God all throughout our days to lead a fruitful life effectively and remain free from the deadly effects of sinful weeds. By partnering with the Spirit on an ongoing basis and talking to God through the Holy Spirit about anything and everything that comes up in our day, we effectively receive the living water to wash away our impurities, fill us to the measure with the fullness of Christ, water us with His nourishing word, and refresh us with His presence. Partnering with the Spirit will also provide us with His abundant light to give us wisdom, counsel, understanding, and illumination to show us which way to go if we get lost and need help finding our way out of a situation.

There are several messages that we should take away from this section of our study as it relates to destructive forces.

- Satan is alive and well and will try to deceive anyone, even the people closest to God.
- If Satan could deceive Adam and Even in their undefiled and created state, he is certainly crafty enough to deceive us. We must be on guard and watching for his cunning deception.
- Those close to us can sometimes entice us to sin even if they don't intend to make us suffer any consequences. We must be alert to this possibility and help them to prevent their sin before it penetrates our own soil.

Relatable Bible Figures

Martha and Mary

In Luke 10, the Bible introduces us to two sisters, Martha and Mary, who teach us a valuable lesson about our focus on Christ. Martha had opened her home to Jesus, and after his arrival, her sister Mary was mesmerized by Him and sat at His feet listing to what He said. According to the Bible, Martha was distracted by all the preparations and didn't stop to listen to Jesus. She continued her work and grew aggravated at her sister for not helping. Finally, when she had enough, she went to Jesus and asked, "Lord, don't you care that my sister has left me to do the work by myself? Tell her to help me!"

What was Jesus' response to her in Luke 10:41–42?

_____

Does this scenario sound familiar? No doubt you have been Martha at times. I know I have. We get so distracted by the demands around us that we tend to lose the single focus that is needed. When we allow frustrations and irritations to enter our soil, we cannot focus our attention on God, and we then slow down our ability to bear fruit. The pull of such demands becomes a destructive force. In fact, anything that removes our focus from God can destroy our fruit production if we allow it to happen.

Think for a moment about the fruit of the Spirit as written in Galatians 5:22. We will cover this concept in great detail in the next chapter, but I think it is important to go there now in advance of that study as it will help in your understanding of this topic. As listed in the Bible, the fruit of the Spirit is love, joy, peace, patience, kindness, goodness, faithfulness, gentleness, and self-control. Our goal is such healthy spiritual growth that the fruit grows in abundance in our lives every day. But if we allow ourselves to become irritated by a coworker or spouse who isn't doing his or her share of the work, a child who's screaming in public, or even the weather—complaining that it's too hot in the summer and too cold in the winter—then we lose your ability to be fruitful that day. We can't be irritated at a spouse and yet be overflowing with love. We can't complain about anything and still be filled with joy and peace.

We could go down the list with many examples, but I don't think it's necessary. I'm sure you get the point. As a Christian following the path established for you, this will surely be one of your greatest challenges, but it should be something that you work on each and every day. Make sure you always choose what is better, and the fruit will not be taken away from you.

Reflection

Think of the people who have a negative influence on your life. The list should not only include the ones who intentionally try to lead you to sinfulness, but also any person who causes anxiety and stress by their actions.

Pray that God will clarify for you who in your life is a true negative influence, rather than those we struggle with in our hearts for other reasons that may be of our own flesh.

Write your list of pests and why they are pests below. Remember, what you write here is personal and will not be shared. Use additional paper if necessary.

_____

_____

_____

_____

Now commit to action to keep the pests, or at least their influences, at a distance from your spiritual growth. It's likely that in most cases, you will still have to associate with these individuals, but even so, you don't have to be affected negatively by them. Ask for God's help in effectively dealing with the anxiety they are causing. If the person is an intentional pest and is part of your social life, you must make the decision to remove the source of the negative influence permanently. Talk to the pest and calmly explain why his or her influence is affecting you negatively and why you feel a change is necessary. Ask God for help with this conversation, and he will certainly provide His assistance. Of course, pray for the pest and, if necessary, introduce the person to Christ. Nothing fixes a problem person more quickly than becoming friends with the Prince of Peace.

Blessed Assurances

- God is stronger than all destructive forces combined.

- God offers Himself as a barrier and shield against the world and its negative influences.

- Christian friends play a vital role in insulating against the same world and influenes

- Understand that God may have plans to use you as fertilizer; Embrace the fact that you were chosen to fulfill part in His master plan. Know that when His plan is complete, your joyous testimony will make up the fertilizer that will help others.

- Absolutely nothing can penetrate the armor of God. Wear it continually!

Fertilize Yourself:

2 Peter 1:3-9 instructs us in the following to "make our calling and election sure":

His divine power has given us everything we need for life and godliness through our knowledge of him who called us by his own glory and goodness. Through these he has given us his very great and precious promises, so that through them you may participate in the divine nature and escape the corruption in the world caused by evil desires.

For this very reason, make every effort to add to your faith goodness; and to goodness, knowledge; and to knowledge, self-control; and to self-control, perseverance; and to perseverance, godliness; and to godliness, brotherly kindness; and to brotherly kindness, love. For if you possess these qualities in increasing measure, they will keep you from being ineffective and unproductive in your knowledge of our Lord Jesus Christ. But if anyone does not have them, he is nearsighted and blind, and has forgotten that he has been cleansed from his past sins.

Therefore, my brothers, be all the more eager to make your calling and election sure. For if you do these things, you will never fall, and you will receive a rich welcome into the eternal kingdom of our Lord and Savior Jesus Christ."

Essentially, this passage of scripture outlines how you can take good virtues and add to them more good virtues in order and increasing in number until you have achieved a state of being that keeps your spiritual growth from being ineffective and unproductive, and subsequently can assure you a rich welcome in heaven to dwell eternally.

In much the same way, many other verses of the Bible document precepts that will provide you a gain if you practice them in increasing number and, in contrast, many more verses list the things you should not do. This list includes any seed that could possibly form roots in your garden and choke out your beautiful blessings.

For this chapter's fertilization exercise, spend some time considering the virtues, or precepts, present in your life versus the weeds that might crop up on any given day. Seek consciously to add to the precepts in increasing number and decrease the number of forming weeds. If you notice a sequence or trend where you are seeing a weed continually present know that roots are forming or have already formed; you must ask God to remove the weeds from your life by the roots. Actively work with God as He seeks to do this in your life. To help you, below is a list of Virtues/Precepts and Weeds as directly found in the Bible to use as a reference.

Virtues/Precepts	Weeds
Love	Greed
Joy	Anxiety
Peace	Submission to Society
Patience	Conceit or Pride
Kindness	Provocation
Gentleness	Sexual Immorality or Impurity
Self-Control	Hatred
Faith	Discord
Humility	Jealousy or Envy
Compassion	Rage or easy Anger
Forgiveness	Malice
Thankfulness	Selfish Ambition
Mercy	Dissensions
Purity	Drunkenness
Obedience	Fear
Forgiveness	Filthy Language
Honesty	Gossiping
Persistence in doing Good	Foolish Controversies
Honor others above self / Selflessness	Revenge
Consideration of others	Arrogance
Indwelling of God's Word	Quarreling
Use of Spiritual Gifts	Resentment
Submission to Husband	Idolatry
Wholehearted Service to the Lord	Favoritism
Continual prayer	Slander
Respect for Others	Boasting / Bragging
Fear of God	Rudeness
Honor to Parents	Rebelling against Authority
Perseverance	Being swayed by false prophets
Hospitality	Exasperating Children
Trustworthiness	Lying

In the same way, also spend time this week identifying those people in your life who may be keeping you from the level of abundant growth you are seeking. This group should not only include ones who intentionally try to lead you into sinfulness but also any person who causes you anxiety and stress. Now commit to action to keep the pests, or at least their influences at a distance from your spiritual growth. It's likely that you will still have to work with or associate with these individuals, but even so, you don't have to be negatively affected by them. And of course, pray for that person and the negative influence they are having on you. Ask God to help guide you in every step and interaction you take with such people. You may be the positive influence that He uses to change their life, but always take that direction from Him.

Remember, this project takes dedication and effort, but the harvest you will reap from your sowing will be well worth the time spent.

Chapter Six: Reaping the Harvest

Foundation Scriptures

"But the fruit of the Spirit is love, joy, peace, patience, kindness, goodness, faithfulness, gentleness and self-control." (Galatians 5:22–23)

"The one who sows to please the Spirit, from the Spirit will reap eternal life. Let us not become weary in doing good, for at the proper time we will reap a harvest if we do not give up." (Galatians 6:8–9)

Introduction

In this chapter, we will focus on not one, but two foundation scriptures. Each has great relevance to our study, and both refer to the harvest that we will reap as a result of our spiritual growth.

Our first foundation scripture shows us what we can expect to achieve if we follow a path of spiritual growth as outlined in this study. But that is not all God has in store for us. The second scripture reminds us that we will not only reap an earthly harvest full of rich blessings and spiritual wellness, we will also receive a heavenly harvest in which we shall inherit the kingdom of heaven.

$\mathscr{D}$efinitions

Physical Harvest

-noun

1. a crop or yield of one growing season.
2. a supply of anything gathered at maturity and stored: *a harvest of wheat.*
3. the result or consequence of any act, process, or event: *The journey yielded a harvest of wonderful memories.*

To Harvest Physically

-verb

1. to gather (a crop or the like); reap.
2. to gather the crop from: *to harvest the fields.*
3. to gather, win, acquire, or use (a prize, product, or result of any past act, process, plan, et cetera.
4. to catch, take, or remove for use: *Fishermen harvested hundreds of salmon from the river.*

Source: Unabridged Random House Dictionary

Spiritual Harvest

-noun

1. the crop or yield of fruit of the Spirit following abundant spiritual growth
2. the supply of fruit of the Spirit stored for sharing with others as a reflection of God's presence in your life
3. the fruitfulness resulting from following a spiritual path according to God's Word
4. Christ's ascent to heaven as firstfruit
5. the rapture during which Christ will harvest His believers

To Harvest Spiritually

-verb

1. to reap a positive result after sowing a positive effort
2. to gain or acquire fruitfulness as a result of abundant spiritual growth
3. to gather believers at the time of the rapture as a harvest of souls

Scripture Study: Harvesting the Fruit of the Word

<u>Putting it All Together</u>

• What it takes to have a spiritual harvest

Stop and consider something for a minute. Is it possible to be part of an earthly harvest and not a heavenly harvest? In contrast, is it possible to be part of a heavenly harvest and not an earthly harvest? To answer that question, let's first look at what it takes to be part of the heavenly harvest.

Read John 3:16, Acts 16:13, Romans 10:9, and John 20:31. What do they all have in common?

_____

_____

Being saved means that we have accepted Christ as your personal Lord and Savior and marks us as one who will have everlasting life, either though ongoing life after death or through the harvest that will happen as part of the rapture. Either way, we are guaranteed the promise of eternal life and all the blessings that go along with that life if we simply believe in Christ as God, the Son.

This should help answer at least one of the questions posed above. No, it is not possible to be part of an earthly harvest and not a heavenly harvest because both require that we believe. If we fail to believe truly in Him and His promises, we can't experience either harvest. If we do believe in Him and His promises, then we automatically are included in the heavenly harvest and are able to receive an earthly harvest, but will not automatically receive it.

Why isn't the earthly harvest automatic? That's because we choose our own destiny on Earth and because Satan is slipping in and out of every corner of our garden, attempting to contaminate it. Through our free will and his temptations, we as humans are prone to sin. Some of us sin more, some sin less, but we all sin. The degree to which we do so in contrast to the degree to which we practice those disciplines necessary for spiritual growth, determines whether we will have an abundant harvest.

You can be a Christian who truly believes and will ultimately go to heaven with other believers, but you can, at the same time, lead a life that bears little or no fruit. As a result, you miss out on some great blessings that God would like to shower on you. Just as a parent should not provide rewards to a defiant child, God will not provide blessings to a defiant believer. And although His love is unfailing, God sometimes has to use discipline to help us realize that we are missing out on a lot in our relationship with Him if we do not change our ways. As a gardener trims and prunes a plant, God will do the same for us when he sees that we are not growing properly.

What does John 15:1 say about how we are trimmed and pruned and why trimming and pruning are necessary?

_____

_____

Are there distracting areas in your life that provide no value and certainly do not fit in with God's will...a will always consistent with activities worthy of His glory? If so, you can be assured that God will make it ever-apparent that these areas serve no use in your life and will at some point effectively eliminate them. In doing so, He will promote an even greater spiritual growth with results that will often surprise you.

In addition to trimming and pruning us, God also uses two other techniques to help us grow fruit of spiritual quality: grafting and rooting. Grafting in nature is the process of uniting a shoot or bud with a growing plant by insertion or by placing in close contact. The goal is to produce growth, hardiness, soil tolerance, and compatibility to produce a higher quality and quantity of fruit. To ensure a successful grafting process, there must be maximum contact between the inner layers of both the original plant and the graft so that they grow together successfully. This grafting process allows for A good example of this is seen in North American grape roots grafted with grape vines from Europe which allows the European grapes to be grown in areas infested with *Phylloxera*, a soil-dwelling insect that attacks and kills European grapes when grown on their own roots. The North American roots grafted in provide great protection from a force that would otherwise cause destruction to the vine.

This grafting is similar to what God does for us. He grafts us into Himself by inserting in us His Holy Spirit so that we will have His roots and have a natural protection against the destructive forces that we discussed in the previous chapter. God uses grafting to produce our spiritual fruitfulness as well as to protect us.

How does He do this?

The answer is found in Romans 11.

Read Romans 11 to find the correct answers to the following questions.

Why did God break off the branches of the Israelites?

- ☐ The Israelites were disobedient, unbelieving, and rejected God.
- ☐ The Israelites were so obedient that God wanted to transplant them to form other fruitful trees.
- ☐ The Israelites broke themselves off to show their faithfulness to Christ.
- ☐ God accidentally broke the Israelites' branches.

Whom did God graft into the space where the branches were broken off?

- ☐ remnants of obedient Israelites, as a reward
- ☐ disobedient Israelites, as a means of salvation
- ☐ Gentiles, as a means of reward
- ☐ Gentiles, because of their faith

How did Paul refer to the Gentiles in Romans 11:17?

☐ a fruitful olive tree ☐ a sturdy olive branch
☐ a wild olive shoot ☐ a flavorful olive

Why did God graft the Gentiles into Himself?

☐ so they could share in the nourishing sap from His root
☐ to make the Israelites jealous
☐ to show the Gentiles His mercy
☐ all of the above

What warning was given to the Gentiles?

☐ not to show boastfulness or arrogance because this might cause them to be broken off, just like the Israelites
☐ not to associate with any Israelites because they might become corrupted
☐ not to spread the gospel because they might not fully understand what they were teaching
☐ not to eat holy bread because it might contain some unholy ingredients

Did Paul say the branches that were broken off could never part of God again?

☐ Yes—he said that the branches would be removed and then burned.
☐ No—he said that the branches could be grafted back in after six years.
☐ No—he said the branches could be grafted back in if the Isrealites reconciled with him and believed.
☐ No—he said the branches would be automatically grafted back in after the Gentiles had successfully taken root with God.

Again, remember that the analogies and teachings in the New Testament were written with a dual purpose: direct applicability to those whom the authors were teaching at the time and as a message to those who would read them in the future.

Here is a summary of what we can learn from Romans 11.

- God wants us to be part of Him, and He is willing to graft us in despite the fact that we might be wild shoots (sinners).

- God chose us to be grafted in not by our acts, but by His grace.

- If we choose not to believe and become disobedient to God, our grafted branch will be broken off.

- If we return to God in faith and belief, we will be grafted back on because of His mercy.

- When we have been successfully grafted in with God and have His roots, we will bear holy fruit.

As previously mentioned, the second notable method of multiplying growth to produce quality fruit is by rooting. Through rooting, a cutting or piece of the parent plant is cut and stuck into soil where it can grow roots from the buried portion to become a complete plant. Most fruit trees cannot be reproduced by this process, but a few, like the olive and fig trees, can. (It's interesting to note that not only does scientific research into rooting identify these two specific trees as examples of the few trees that can be multiplied through rooting, the Bible also uses these two trees symbolically.)

The most notable use of the rooting process in the Bible is found in the book of Ezekiel in chapter 17, verses 22–24. In this chapter, God is speaking to the Israelites through a parable He gave to Ezekiel to present to them regarding their disobedience. At the conclusion of this parable, Ezekiel notes the following: ***This is what the Sovereign LORD says: I myself will take a shoot from the cedar and plant it; I will break off a tender sprig from its topmost shoots and plant it on a high and lofty mountain. On the mountain heights of Israel I will plant it; it will produce branches and bear fruit and become a splendid cedar. Birds of every kind will nest in it; they will find shelter in the shade of its branches. All the trees of the field will know that I the LORD bring down the tall tree and make the low tree grow tall. I dry up the green tree and make the dry tree flourish. I the LORD have spoken, and I will do it.***

This passage has great meaning for us today. As written, it was meant to prophesy the coming of the Messiah and all that Christ would bring to the world. Using imagery, God was stating that He would break a holy piece of Himself off and plant it on earthly soil in Israel. God further noted that this shoot would grow to produce branches, bear fruit, and become a splendid cedar. Why did he use cedar as an example? Because of the properties of evergreens. They grow very strong and tall with many sturdy branches. This describes the sheltering nature of Jesus, which will provide us protection and shade. As we seek shelter from the devastating effects of the human life, the promise that God broke off a part of himself as a means of promoting our future fruitfulness should be very reassuring. In doing so, He secured not only the promise of Christ, but also the promise of the Holy Spirit, in which we have access to the nourishing fruit that will help to help us get through all of our struggles.

- Ensuring Growth

God gave us clear instructions on how to have abundant spiritual growth that will lead to an incredible harvest. The unfortunate reality, however, is that many of us fail to use all the instructions consistently and often fail to produce the abundance of fruit that we might otherwise receive. Many, in fact, not only fail to follow the instructions, we also fail even to understand the need for instructions. Some simply don't realize that a spiritual harvest can exist and that we can abundantly grow fruit of the Spirit. And in doing so, those individuals miss the chance to have overflowing quantities of love, joy, peace, patience, gentleness, kindness, goodness, faithfulness, and self-control in their lives. To miss out on all these benefits is to miss out on a huge, transformative opportunity. Yet many people go a lifetime without ever experiencing this type of abundance. So what are we to do to ensure that we are not among the unfortunate who miss out on this incredible blessing?

Let's look at our first foundation scripture again and notice two focal points. First, notice how the singular form of *fruit* is used even though there are nine different characteristics listed. Although often incorrectly described as fruit*s* of the Spirit, it isn't referring to many fruits, but to one single fruit. Why is it singular? Because of the law of nature that makes it impossible for a tree to bear more than one type of fruit. Evidence of this is found in Genesis 1:11–12.

What does God command the seed-bearing plants and trees on the land to bear?

- ☐ fruits with seeds in it, according to their various kinds

- ☐ fruit with seed in it, according to their singular kind

- ☐ fruit with seed in it, according to their various kinds

- ☐ fruits with seeds in it, according to their singular kind

Yes, there are many varieties of plants and trees, but they all produce fruit according to what they are. Apple trees only produce apples and never produce oranges or orange seeds. The fruit listed in Galatians 5 comes from the Spirit and only the Spirit; therefore, it is a single source and type of fruit.

Second, we must understand that the nine components listed do not create the fruit, but that the Spirit creates them. This means that if you live your life according to the disciplines we've discussed as necessary for abundant spiritual growth, you will have fruitfulness in the end. That fruitfulness consists of love, joy, peace, patience, kindness, goodness, faithfulness, gentleness, and self-control. These components are all byproducts of leading a life fully directed towards God and not present in their pure form in any other type of life.

Basically, what this scripture tells us is that if we live according to the Spirit, we will have an abundance of love, joy, peace, patience, kindness, goodness, faithfulness, gentleness, and self-control. We will be spiritually well and will have an earthly existence that is full and abundant according to Scripture, and we will be blessed because these are the blessings He gives.

To grow spiritual fruit, however, we must consistently walk in obedience to what we've been studying in order to achieve success. Let's review the steps necessary to achieve abundant fruitfulness.

The following are the actions we must take to be abundantly fruitful:

1. Maintain pure soil by sifting out all negative components through the Word of Truth.

2. Allow God to plant seeds in our lives and acknowledge our role in caring for the seeds jointly with him as the Master Gardener

3. Make sure we receive plenty of Living Water by immersing ourselves in prayer, communion, and the Word; Repent of our sins to receive cleansing.

4. Make sure we receive plenty of light to illuminate our path as we seek direction; Make sure we are also a light for others.

5. Allow God to be an internal foundation/barrier to prevent the formation of weeds.

6. Ensure adequate mulch around ourselves through Christian Fellowship and accountability to be an external barrier against weeds

7. Keep repellant on through the armor of God to help control the effects of pests.

8. Fertilize ourselves regularly and allow ourselves to serve as fertilizer.

9. Allow ourselves to be trimmed and pruned.

10. Appreciate the Master Gardener through praise and referrals!

According to John 15: 4, what else does Jesus say is necessary to bear fruit? Why?

_____

_____

What does John 15:6 say will happen to those who do not remain in him?

_____

In contrast, what promise is given to those who remain in Christ and allow His Word to remain in them, according to John 15:7?

_____

_____

John 15:8 covers step number ten and notes that when we bear fruit, the result is that He, the Father, is glorified, and we show ourselves as disciples. Let's stop for a moment to consider these two facts. First, the Father is glorified. As defined, *glorify* means to magnify, extol, or praise God and to acknowledge Him as to His being, attributes, and acts. That's exactly what He wants and expects from us. Remember, God's will in everything is that everything glorifies Him. Thus, as we previously covered, an answered prayer occurs when we align our requests to God's will and ultimately His glorification rather than self-centered satisfaction of our immediate wants.

God is especially pleased when we bear fruit because it shows that we acknowledge Him and what He has done for us. But that isn't all He is pleased about when we bear fruit. He is also pleased that we show ourselves as disciples. Some people relate the word *disciples* to the word *apostles* and think of the twelve disciples of Christ, who were disciples *and* apostles. Here's the difference between the two. The apostles were the early followers of Jesus who carried the Christian message into the world. Disciples, by definition, are pupils who learn and then practice what they learn. Yes, the apostles were disciples, and we are correct in referring to them as such, but we are also disciples if we follow Christ's teachings. What does this definition say in relation to our spiritual fruitfulness? It says that if we are obedient to God's commands, we will be bear spiritual fruit; it will, thus, be apparent that we are disciples.

Remember, eliminating the chance that our garden will not produce fruit takes effort. Ensuring that our garden will produce abundant fruit takes significant work. We can be assured, though, that every ounce of energy that we put into this effort will be worth it.

Read the following scriptures and fill in the missing word.

"Therefore, since we are surrounded by such a great cloud of witnesses, let us throw off everything that hinders and the sin that so easily entangles, and let us run with _____ the race marked out for us." (Hebrews 12:1)

"You need to _____ so that when you have done the will of God, you will receive what he has promised." (Hebrews 10:36)

"Blessed is the man who _____ under trial, because when he has stood the test, he will receive the crown of life that God has promised to those who love him." (James 1:12)

"As you know, we consider blessed those who have _____. You have heard of Job's _____ and have seen what the Lord finally brought about. The Lord is full of compassion and mercy." (James 5:11)

"(Love) always protects, always trusts, always hopes, always _____." (1 Corinthians 13:7)

"Therefore, since we have been justified through faith, we have peace with God through our Lord Jesus Christ, through whom we have gained access by faith into this grace in which we now stand. And we rejoice in the hope of the glory of God. Not only so, but we also rejoice in our sufferings, because we know that suffering produces _____ ; _____, character; and character, hope. And hope does not disappoint us, because God has poured out his love into our hearts by the Holy Spirit, whom he has given us." (Romans 5:1–5)

"Consider it pure joy, my brothers, whenever you face trials of many kinds, because you know that the testing of your faith develops _____. _____ must finish its work so that you may be mature and complete, not lacking anything." (James 1:2–4)

As you see, perseverance is a requirement if we expect to receive the fullness of all God has in store for us as His children. What specifically must we persevere to do? We must not only persevere to share the message about Christ, we must also persevere to follow the path God has for us and consistently attend our garden as the Master Gardener simultaneously tends to it.

To promote our continued perseverance, let's review a few more scriptures that relate to the ten steps to abundant fruitfulness that we studied previously. These scriptures will help prevent our failure as they promote our growth.

How does Philippians 4:49 say you can keep your soil pure and ultimately acquire peace?

_____

_____

How do the following scriptures describe God's love, which is a component of holy seeds?

See Exodus 15:13, Psalm 6:4, Psalm 13:5, Psalm 21:7, Psalm 31:16, Psalm 32:10, Psalm 33:5, Psalm 33:18, Psalm 36:7, Psalm 44:26, Psalm 48:9, Psalm 51:1, Psalm 52:8, Psalm 85:7, Psalm 9:14, Psalm 107:8, 15, 21, and 31; Psalm 119:41, Psalm 119:76, Psalm 130:7, Psalm 143:8, Psalm 143:12, Psalm 147:11, Isaiah 54:10, Lamentations 3:32, and Hosea 10:12.

_____

_____

What does Deuteronomy 22:9 say we should remember when planting seeds?

_____

This means that we can't plant both seeds for God and for man. All our seeds should be for and of God.

How do we receive rain in its season to bear fruit for harvest, according to Leviticus 26:3?

_____

What does Matthew 7 say we need to keep up with if we are to produce fruit?

_____

How do you achieve the fruit of the light, according to Ephesians 5:8–10?

_____

_____

What does Ephesians 5:11 say you should do with fruitless deeds of the darkness?

_____

What do both Proverbs 18:20 and Hebrews 13:15 say about praising God?

_____

_____

How can we be assured that we can become fruitful, according to John 15:16?

_____

How to Recognize Fruitfulness

• Fruit of the Spirit is abundantly visible

There are two simple questions we need to answer as we move forward in our understanding of fruit as it applies to our lives. Where do red apples come from, and how do you know red apples are abundantly present?

Well, of course, red apples come from a red apple tree, and we know they are abundantly present when there are red apples on and around the red apple tree! I wasn't trying to insult your intelligence or leave you with a riddle, but to make the point that the fruit of the Spirit can only come from the Spirit. We sometimes try to place ourselves in the equation and assume that if we behave outwardly in a loving, joyful, peaceful, patient, kind, good, faithful, gentle, or self-controlled way, we are bearing fruit. But we are not. We cannot simply behave in a certain way to be fruitful. We can only be fruitful if we have spiritual growth to the degree that the Spirit produces the fruit from our inner being.

The second part of the question addresses the abundance of our fruitfulness. You can't say that an apple tree has produced fruit when there are only blossoms. And you can't say there is abundant fruit when there are buds or even unripe, small, green apples on the tree. There is a promise of fruit when blossoms and buds are present, but one cannot say there is the presence of abundant fruit until it is physically present. In the same manner, we cannot say there is the full presence of fruit of the Spirit until it...and He... is present in our lives in abundance.

Essentially, after we have grown spiritually in the manner that we've described in our study of the Word including, but not limited to, ridding ourselves of negative actions and thoughts that take up space that should be reserved for God, we then will begin to grow fruit. And with persistence in our faith and belief, and patience in our hope and trust, our fruitfulness will become abundant.

Think for a moment about someone you know who exemplifies each fruit of the Spirit ... someone who is known for having abundant love, joy, peace, patience, kindness, goodness, faithfulness, gentleness, and self-control. What makes the person as he or she is? Your answer will most certainly include the words attributed to godliness, such as the Christ-like actions that are present in such a person's life. You recognize them because of their fruit, but the fruit isn't a result of their outward characteristics; it's because of their inward faith, obedience, and actions.

Translating this principle to our own lives, we know that if we want to have abundant fruit of the spirit—to be like the people who never seem to worry in a season of drought and always seem to bear fruit—we must then focus on our spiritual growth through faith including hope and trust, obedience through prayer and following God's commands, and finally through our actions as discussed in the ten steps above. When you do finally experience an abundance of fruit in your life, you will essentially have exchanged all of the negative, dark things in your life for those that can only be provided by the grace of God.

Review Galatians 5:22 and fill in the fruit of the Spirit below based on what you will be receiving in exchange for a negative attribute or behavior.

Hatred for _____

Sorrow for _____

Anxiety for _____

Impatience for _____

Anger for _____

Wickedness for _____

Faithlessness for _____

Harshness for _____

Unrestraint for _____

When you experience this exchange, your experience through the long, often difficult journey of life will be much different. Trust me when I say the sights you see on your new journey will be nothing like your previous journey, sometimes filled with darkness and despair. *You* will be like a tree planted by the water that sends out its roots by the stream. *You* will not fear when heat comes; *your* leaves will always be green. *You* will have no worries in a year of drought, and *you* will never fail to bear fruit.

- Blessings shower from above

There are few things that thrill me more about my life than the blessings that God showers upon me. It's not because I'm selfishly seeking good things from Him to make my life better, but because within His blessings, I see a glimpse Him and His great love for me. No one else can ever love me unconditionally the way God does, and He continues to bless me even when I don't seem worthy. Much to my delight, I've noticed that in the times of my life when fruit of the Spirit is abundantly present, blessings are present also. And to be clear, the blessings aren't generally of a tangible nature, but instead are the blessing of Him that can only be understood and fully received upon the experience of knowing Him.

Read the following scriptures and note the promise of blessings that are written.

Psalm 128

_____

_____

1 Corinthians 9:23

_____

Ephesians 1:3

_____

Enhancing the Fruitfulness of Others

- Sharing your harvest

Once you have experienced true, abundant fruitfulness, it's impossible to keep it to yourself. You find the abundance overflowing in your everyday life and others can visibly see that fruit. You'll also likely feel compelled to tell others about it. God knows this will happen and, as part of His plan, uses our praise to Him and about Him to result in many more Christians being fruitfully brought into His kingdom. Therefore, He encourages us to share our harvest.

In Psalm 78:4, according to David, whom will we tell of the praiseworthy deeds of the Lord, his power, and the wonders he has done?

_____

What does Colossians tell us the gospel is doing all over the world?

_____

And so the Gospel has spread. Stories of God, of Christ, and of the Holy Spirit have indeed been passed down from generation to generation because of abundant fruitfulness that could not be contained. And not just any fruitfulness, but fruitfulness that is attributed to God, His power and His wonders … hence, fruit of the Spirit.

- Cross-pollination

As you might already know, cross-pollination is a wonderful miracle of God by which pollen from one flower combines with the underdeveloped seeds of another to produce developed seeds that will grow into more fruit. As defined, figurative cross-pollination is a sharing or interchange of knowledge and ideas for mutual enrichment. The Holy Spirit uses spiritual synergy to accomplish cross-pollination by sharing information, knowledge, or thoughts with us to use for the enrichment of another.

What is spiritual synergy? Synergy itself, by definition, is the interaction of two or more agents or forces so that their combined effect is greater than the sum of their individual effects. Spiritually, it is the interaction of two or more people with the same Holy Spirit acting on behalf of at least one of them to achieve an effect greater than either would have produced together without the Holy Spirit. As part of sharing your harvest with others, it is where God enables you, through the Spirit within you, to have insight into the needs of others so you can offer your fruit to them to help nourish their souls. Have you ever had someone unexpectedly pop into your mind and found out later about a crisis that person had been experiencing? Or been awakened from a deep sleep to pray for someone and later find that the person was ill and in need of prayers? Have you been led to send an uplifting e-mail to an acquaintance, only to get a reply of appreciation noting that the recipient really needed that boost right at that moment? These events can and do happen through our sensitivity to the Holy Spirit. Through your individual obedience and the resulting fruitfulness, God may recognize you as the perfect person to help another and will use you for that purpose. It might only be in a fleeting moment when you say a prayer for a stranger whom you pass on the street, but the Spirit will prompt you to say that prayer.

What does Romans 1:11–12 command us to do? Why?

_____

_____

_____

But spiritual synergy is actually deeper than just using a faithful person to help others. I saved the discussion for here because I want you to comprehend fully the potential magnitude of God's power and grace in your life and in the lives of others. Because spiritual synergy is the process by which the same Holy Spirit in dwelling in two persons works for the greater good of at least one of the two individuals, it can be a very powerful process. In fact, many Christian testimonies develop out of spiritual synergy.

In my case, for example, a woman a thousand miles away from me felt compelled to give her child up for adoption even though her supportive family begged her to keep the child. The Spirit led her to the name *Leah* before she met me. The same Spirit led me to contact the same adoption agency she had contacted, and to check my voicemail on the fateful day when I first heard of our baby girl. The same Spirit led both of us to say *"yes"* to being matched for adoption. How do I know this was the Spirit? Because all of these events defied the odds. Even the timeframe of three weeks to be matched and four months to hold my newborn child was a near-impossible statistic amid the standard waiting time of two years.

Why does God take such measures as using spiritual synergy to affect our lives and the lives of others positively? Both because this leads more people to know Him; and because of His incredible love for us as part of His adopted family which includes those who have chosen to believe in His Son. After having adopted Emily, this gives greater meaning to me. We don't love Emily more than we do our biological children, but we appreciate the fact that she was chosen to be ours. I'm sure that's very similar to the love God has for us. He chose us, and we subsequently chose His son and therefore received the adoption. For me, that choice raises the emphasis on the word *cross* in *cross-pollination*. And it certainly makes me eternally grateful for my decision to be part of this adopted family because of the cross that continues to pollinate my life each and every day.

Relational Bible Figures

Jesus: The Firstfruit

The final part of our study together brings us to the one and only Jesus. We conclude with Jesus for two reasons. First, He was and is the firstfruit, which is directly applicable to our study, and second, because every journey we take should conclude with Christ as our destination. He should be our hope from beginning to end.

For this part of the study, we must first look to the Old Testament to find the true meaning behind Christ's designation as the firstfruit. In the process of revealing His plan of salvation for mankind, God established annual holy days around the harvest seasons and this is where our understanding of firstfruits originated. Firstfruits, by definition, are the first agricultural products to ripen. On the same general principal that every firstborn man belonged to God and was to be devoted to him, the firstfruits, including the first grain to ripen each season, were to be brought as an offering to God. To accomplish this, the Israelites celebrated a Feast of the Firstfruits during which the Israelites dedicated the first ripened stalks of grain to God in anticipation of a greater harvest to come. This feast was actually one of several feasts, all of which served a purpose to demonstrate obedience by the Israelites. But perhaps even more significant than the purpose these feasts served at the time, they also were created to share a prophetic and symbolic message to mankind for the duration of the earth.

Although our study focuses on fruits, I think it is important that you understand the symbolic nature of all of the feasts to help you internalize all the magnificence of God and His ultimate plans for you.

Let's start by looking at what the Bible had to say in the Old Testament about the feasts.

According to Leviticus 23, who established these feasts? _____

Read the entire chapter of Leviticus 23 and fill in the name of the feast below. Take some time to meditate on the prophetic significance of each feast as identified by biblical scholars and recognize the significance of what this means for us today, knowing that we are living in a time where all of the prophecies according to the feasts have yet to be fulfilled.

Feast	Timing	Purpose	Prophetic Significance
	The fourteenth day of the first month at twilight	Passover was meant to commemorate Isreal's deliverance from Egypt, including the 'passover' by which Jews were spared the death of their firstborn through the blood of a lamb placed above their door.	This feast represents Jesus as our Passover, the Lamb of God who was sacrificed, and whose blood was received and applied so the wrath of God would pass us over. It speaks of redemption as a result of Jesus dying on the cross for our sins. This prophetic statement was complete when Jesus died on the cross on the exact day of the Feast of Passover.
	The fifteenth day of each month for seven days	This feast showed the purity Israel was to walk in (illustrated by eating only bread without leaven, a type of sin) after the blood-deliverance of Passover.	This feast relates to the time of Jesus' burial during which he as received by God as holy and complete. It speaks of sanctification. Jesus was set apart. His body would not decay in the grave. This prophetic statement was complete when Jesus was placed in a tomb during the Feast of Unleavened Bread.

The day following the Passover's Sabbath	This feast was a time to give the firstfruits of harvest to God, including the first ripened stalks of grain in anticipation of a greater harvest to come.	The feast of the firstfruits relates to the resurrection of Jesus, who was the first human to receive resurrection. It speaks of the Lord's triumphant resurrection in which death simply could not hold her foe. This prophetic statement was complete on the third day when Jesus rose victoriously from the grave, which was, in fact, on the day of the Feast of the Firstfruits.
Fifty days after the seventh Sabbath.	This feast signified the completion of the wheat harvest and Israelites were to bring a new grain offering to the Lord.	This feast symbolizes Jesus giving us the gift of the Holy Spirit which inaugurated the New Covenant and Church Age. It speaks of origination signifying our origin as being from Christ when we are reborn. This prophetic statement was complete when the Holy Spirit was given on the exact day of the Feast of Weeks.
The first day of the seventh month (which was also the first day of the first month of the Hebrew calendar).	This feast was a day of rest with a memorial blowing of trumpets to begin ten days of awe before the Day of Atonement in which the Israelites reflected on their sin and the need for atonement.	This feast symbolizes the rapture of the church that begins with the sound of a trumpet.

	The fifteenth day of the seventh month	This feast was a time to rejoice in God's deliverance and provision for Israel during the time of wilderness wandering.	This feast is symbolic of the millennium, specifically the rest, peace, and comfort that God will bring us when He delivers us from this earth.

Stop and consider another reason why Jesus should be considered a firstfruit. He was the first man to model the behaviors necessary to produce fruitfulness. These attributes, appropriately termed Christ-like behaviors, comprise the list that you studied at the conclusion of the last chapter. Remember that we will never be able to achieve the high level of purity that Jesus had during his walk on Earth, but we can strive to be like Him in all that we do. In turn, we will follow in His footsteps with our individual fruitfulness.

In summary, understand the significance of Jesus as the firstfruit of the harvest that God has planned for you. By following a path of spiritual growth, you will not only experience fruitfulness on Earth; you will also be guaranteed a fruitful afterlife for all eternity.

Blessed Assurances

- By following a path of spiritual growth, you will experience an earthly harvest according to God's plans and purpose for your life.

- If you persevere to follow the will of God, you will reap great rewards.

- Your personal harvest will include an overflowing abundance of love, joy, peace, patience, kindness, goodness, faithfulness, gentleness, and self-control.

- Belief in Jesus, as the firstfruit, will guarantee you a spiritual harvest in eternity.

Fertilize Yourself For Life

Begin partnering with the Spirit this week, using the attached flowchart as a guide. As you awaken each morning, ask God to be your partner that day to guide you in all truth, knowledge, wisdom, and understanding so your dark path can be lightened. Ask for greater recognition of any behaviors in your day that might be contributing to poor soil conditions, ask Him to plant whatever seeds need to be planted that day, and for continued water to wash away any impurities to help your seeds grow.

Then, throughout the day, when you are faced with any anxiety-causing situation, such as becoming overwhelmed with work or encountering difficulties that you aren't sure how to handle, talk to Him. If Satan begins to tempt you to wander off the path you are on with Christ, ask God to place a shield around you to keep Satan out. Remember, engagement is the reason the Holy Spirit was given to you. As Jesus promised in John 14:26, "the Counselor, the Holy Spirit, whom the Father will send in my name, will teach you all things and will remind you of everything I have said to you. Peace I leave with you; my peace I give you." By communicating intimately with the Holy Spirit within you throughout the day, you will be filled with to the measure with water and light, and you will immediately sense a phenomenal change as your growth accelerates beyond your wildest dreams, leading to the harvest of all harvests.

Oh, how I pray that this study has positively affected your life, Precious One. It is my prayer that you will be able to use all the tools that God gave us in this study to achieve not only a fruitful life, but an abundantly fruitful life: a life filled with fruit of the Spirit!

As we conclude our final study, I encourage you not to leave these gardening tools on a shelf. I implore you to continue your quest to seek God in all that you do and to seek to have pure soil, holy seeds, living water, abundant light, and the absence of weeds and pests forevermore. May you not become weary in doing good, for at the proper time, you *will* reap a harvest if you do not give up.

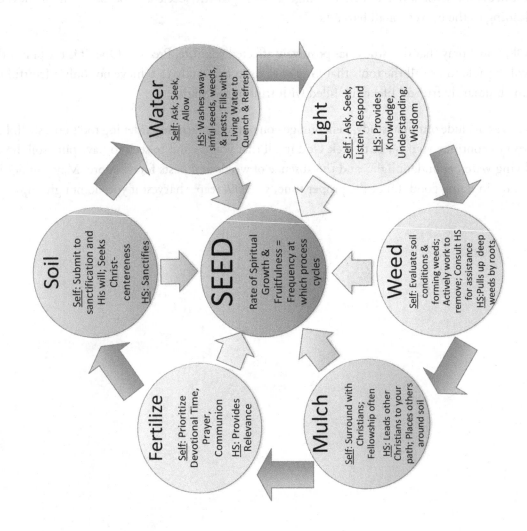

PARTNERING PROCESS

to ensure an abundant harvest

HS = Holy Spirit

Chapter One: Fertile Soil Answer Key

Scripture Study: Sifting through the Word

Read the Parable of the Sower in Matthew 13:3-9 and 18-23.

According to verse 19, what is represented by the soil in which the seed was sown? <u>The heart is represented by the soil in this parable.</u>

According to verse 23, what does the seed falling on good soil represent? <u>The seed falling on good soil represents someone who hears the word and understands it.</u>

How much fruitfulness is produced when a seed is sown in good soil? <u>A hundred, sixty or thirty times what was sown.</u>

Conditions that Establish and Promote Fertile Soil

- Salvation

    According to John 11:25-26, who and what is the source of life? <u>Jesus is the source of life and believing in Him is how we can have life</u>

    According to 1 Corinthians 3:11, who is the only Foundation? <u>Jesus Christ</u>

    Read John 15:1-8. What is required to bear much fruit? <u>Remaining in Christ</u>

    Re-read John 15:1-8 and apply a meaning from each of the above to the blanks below.

    Place: <u>Remain right here </u>in me, as I also <u>remain right here</u> in you.

    Time: Remain <u>now and for all of eternity in me</u>, as I also <u>remain now and for all of eternity</u> in you.

    State: <u>Remain as one, never separate, in me,</u> as I also <u>remain as one, never separate,</u> in you.

- Positional Sanctification

What other verse do you recall in the bible involving blowing to life? <u>Genesis 2:7 Then the Lord God formed a man from the dust of the ground and breathed into his nostrils the breath of life, and the man became a living being.</u>

According to Ephesians 1:4, why did God chose us in Christ before the creation of the world?

<u>For he chose us in him before the creation of the world to be holy and blameless in his sight.</u>

- Relationship

According to the following scriptures, what relationship do we have with God?

John 1:12 <u>We are children of God</u>

Galatians 4:6-7 <u>We are sons (daughters) of God</u>

Romans 8:16 <u>We are God's children</u>

Ephesians 5:1 <u>We are dearly loved children</u>

Why does Ephesians 5:2 say Christ gave Himself up for us as a fragrant offering and sacrifice to God? <u>Christ gave Himself up as a fragrant offering and sacrifice to God because He loved us.</u>

According to John 3:16, how much does God love us?

<u>He loves us enough to give up His one and only Son so we could have eternal life.</u>

Why do we love, according to 1 John 4:19? <u>We love because He first loved us,</u>

According to Romans 8:38-39, what can separate us from the love of God? <u>Nothing can separate us from the love of Christ...neither death nor life, neither angels nor demons, neither the present nor the future, nor any powers, neither height nor depth, nor anything else in all creation will be able to separate us from the love of God that is in Christ Jesus our Lord.</u>

In John 15:9-17, Jesus makes a powerful statement about the love He has for us and how we should love Him and others in order to experience complete joy.

What does this passage also say we are to Christ if we love like He commands?

☐ We are His acquaintances   ☑ We are His friends   ☐ We are His followers

The same scripture continues to state that we did not choose Him, but He chose us.

For what reason did Jesus say He chose us? <u>He chose us so that we might go and bear fruit - fruit that will last.</u>

Components of Fertile Soil

- Fertile soil is rich in faith.

  Read Hebrews 11:1. How is faith defined? <u>Faith is being sure of what we hope for and certain of what we do not see.</u>

  2 Chronicles 20:20: <u>I will be upheld.</u>

  Psalm 31:23: <u>I will be preserved.</u>

  Psalm 37:28: <u>I will not be forsaken.</u>

  Psalm 97:10: <u>My life will be guarded and I will be delivered from the hands of the wicked.</u>

  Proverbs 2:8: <u>He will protect my ways.</u>

  Proverbs 28:20: <u>I will be richly blessed.</u>

  Matthew 21:20–22: <u>I can do great things and will receive whatever I ask for in prayer.</u>

  Romans 4:13: <u>I will gain righteousness.</u>

  Romans 5:1: <u>I will have peace.</u>

  Romans 5:2: <u>I will have access to stand in God's grace.</u>

  Galatians 3:9: <u>I will be blessed.</u>

  Galatians 3:14: <u>I will receive the promise of the Spirit.</u>

  Ephesians 3:16–18: <u>Christ will dwell in my heart.</u>

  Ephesians 6:16: <u>I will have a shield to extinguish the flaming arrows of the evil one.</u>

  2 Thessalonians 1:11: <u>My purpose and acts will be fulfilled.</u>

  James 5:15: <u>I will be raised up, made well, and forgiven.</u>

  I Peter 1:5: <u>I will be shielded by God's power.</u>

  According to Matthew 17:20, how much faith do you need have to move mountains? <u>You only need to have faith as small as a mustard seed.</u>

- Fertile soil is rich in hope.

  Read the following verses that describe what will happen to those who hope in the Lord. Write down what will happen to you if you have hope in Him.

  Lamentations 3:25: <u>The Lord will be good to me.</u>

Romans 8:25: <u>I will wait for what I do not have patiently.</u>

Hebrews 6:19: <u>It will be an anchor for my soul, firm and secure.</u>

Hebrews 7:19: <u>I will be drawn nearer to God.</u>

Isaiah 40:31: <u>I will renew my strength; I will soar like wings on Eagles; I will run and not grow weary; I will walk and not be faint.</u>

Read Romans 12:12. What specific instruction does it provide? <u>Be joyful in hope, patient in affliction, and faithful in prayer.</u>

Read Proverbs 23:18. What certainty does this verse provide? <u>There is surely a future hope for me that will not be cut off.</u>

Read Hebrews 10:19-23. What does this verse tell us about how we should hold onto our hope, and why? <u>We must hold onto hope unswervingly because He who promised is faithful.</u>

- Fertile soil is rich in trust.

Carefully and thoughtfully read the foundation scripture for this chapter. What does it say to you?

<u>If I trust in the Lord, I will be blessed. I won't have any reason to fear anything and will always be fruitful, no matter what comes my way.</u>

How early does trust in the Lord begin, according to Psalm 22:9? <u>Trust begins in infancy (when God brings us out of the womb and we are at our mother's breast).</u>

Read the following scriptures and write down what each verse tells you will happen to those who trust in the Lord.

Psalm 22:4: <u>I will be delivered.</u>

Psalm 22:5: <u>I will not be disappointed.</u>

Psalm 28:7: <u>I will be helped.</u>

Psalm 32:10: <u>I will be surrounded by the Lord's unfailing love.</u>

Psalm 33:21: <u>My heart will rejoice.</u>

Psalm 37:3–4: <u>He will give me all of the desires of my heart.</u>

Psalm 40:4: <u>I will be blessed.</u>

Psalm 125:1: <u>I will not be shaken, but will endure forever.</u>

Proverbs 3:4–6: <u>He will make my paths straight.</u>

Proverbs 28:25: <u>I will prosper.</u>

Isaiah 28:16: <u>I will never be dismayed.</u>

Jeremiah 17:7–8: <u>I will be blessed and will never fail to bear fruit.</u>

Daniel 6:23: <u>I will not be wounded.</u>

Nahum 1:7: <u>God will care for me.</u>

Romans 10:11: <u>I will never be put to shame.</u>

Roman 15:13: <u>I will be filled with joy and peace.</u>

Read Psalm 9:10. Why does this verse say we should trust God? <u>We should trust God because He has never forsaken those who trust him.</u>

Isaiah 26:4 also describes why we should trust in the Lord. How is God described in this verse? Why do you think He is described this way? <u>God is described as the rock eternal. He is described this way because He is a firm foundation and solid support for us at all times.</u>

Read Psalm 127. What point does this verse make? What promise does it offer? <u>The Lord must help you build your home and, as a reward, will bless you with children.</u>

How does Psalm 119:9 say you can keep your soil pure? <u>You keep your soil pure by living according to God's word.</u>

<u>Components of Non-Fertile Soil</u>

- Non-fertile soil is laden with <u>fear.</u>

  Fear is a natural reaction to many things in life and the enemy uses it very well to his advantage to stifle our growth. Components of fear can range from actual fears of disaster to fears of what others think. Insecurities are one of the most common devices of fear Satan uses in his schemes against us and God. He knows that if we are insecure, our focus is most often turned inward, making us in a great sense self-centered which always replaces Christ-centeredness. Are insecurities or fears holding you back? Write down some of them below:

  (Subjective, personal response)

- Non-fertile soil is laden with <u>idolatry.</u>

  The word idolatry may conjure up images of ba'al or asherah poles from the ancient days of the Bible, but Satan uses this unhealthy component much craftier today. Idolatry today comes in the form of money, people, and activity, including busyness. We can even be an idol to ourselves through our pride and discontentment. If any of these things apply to you, list them below.

(Subjective, personal response)

- Non-fertile soil is laden with <u>the past.</u>

  Guilt, shame, and regret are three powerful negative emotions that can keep us bound to our past for many years. Are you experiencing these or any other chains from your past that you are unable to let go? If so, note them below.

  (Subjective, personal response)

- Non-fertile soil is that which is laden with <u>anything negative that defines a person.</u> *Do you have any negative emotions or embedded traits that fit this description? If so, describe them below. (Subjective, personal response)*

Reflection

If you currently have fear in your soil, what do Psalm 56:3 and Psalm 112:7 tell you that you should do when you are fearful or afraid? <u>I should "trust in the Lord" when I am fearful or afraid.</u>

Relatable Bible Figure

Paul

What does Paul urge us to do in Ephesians 4:1? <u>Paul urges us to walk in a manner worthy of the calling to which we have been called, with all humility and gentleness, with patience, bearing with one another in love, eager to maintain the unity of the Spirit in the bond of peace.</u>

Paul continues in Ephesians 4 to discuss impurities including some of those negative things we discussed that could be part of non-fertile soil. What does he say we should do to assure these impurities are not present in verses 22-24? <u>We are to put off our old selves, which are being corrupted by its deceitful desires; to be made new in the attitude of our minds; 24 and to put on the new self, created to be like God in true righteousness and holiness.</u>

Evidence of Paul's fear is found in 1 Corinthians 2:1-4. Of what was Paul fearful? Why is that significant? <u>He had great fear and trembling because he knew he wasn't eloquent or wise, but he demonstrated that God's power is far greater than human wisdom.</u>

What did Paul ask for in order to help with his fear in Ephesians 6:19-20? <u>Paul asks for prayer in order that he might declare the gospel fearlessly</u>

Why does Paul tell us we no longer have to fear in Romans 8:14-15? <u>We no longer have to live in fear</u> <u>because we are the children of God, adopted by Him to sonship.</u>

$\mathcal{D}$igging $\mathcal{D}$eeper

Read the following scripture from Jeremiah 29:11 with emphasis on the italicized word. Pause with each to focus on what the scripture is saying to you in the different context. Do you notice a distinct difference in the verse and the promise in each version? Write the difference in the space provided. The first one is done for you.

"For *I* know the plans *I* have for you," declares the Lord, "plans to prosper you and not to harm you, plans to give you hope and a future."
<u>GOD has plans for my life. No one else, anywhere at any time, has the master set of plans.</u>

"For I *know* the plans I have for you," declares the Lord, "plans to prosper you and not to harm you, plans to give you hope and a future."
<u>God KNOWS the specific plans He has in place for me. The plans aren't something yet to be decided.</u> <u>They are already known.</u>

"For I know *the* plans I have for you," declares the Lord, "plans to prosper you and not to harm you, plans to give you hope and a future."
<u>THE plans God has for me are very specific. They are not just "plans," they are "the plans"—the exact</u> <u>plans that will make me prosper and give me hope and a future.</u>

"For I know the *plans* I have for you," declares the Lord, "*plans* to prosper you and not to harm you, *plans* to give you hope and a future."
<u>God has PLANS for me. They aren't just thoughts or suggestions. He has actual plans for how I will</u> <u>prosper and have hope and a future.</u>

"For I know the plans I *have* for you," declares the Lord, "plans to prosper you and not to harm you, plans to give you hope and a future."
<u>God HAS plans for me, which implies that they are something to be had, something concrete that I</u> <u>will be given.</u>

"For I know the plans I have *for* you," declares the Lord, "plans to prosper you and not to harm you, plans to give you hope and a future."
<u>God has plans FOR me, which implies that the plans will be shared with me.</u>

"For I know the plans I have for *you*," declares the Lord, "plans to prosper *you* and not to harm you, plans to give you hope and a future."
<u>God has plans that are intended only for ME. They were created with me in mind and are specific to</u> <u>both the requests I have laid before Him and the will He has for my life.</u>

"For I know the plans I have for you," *declares* **the Lord, "plans to prosper you and not to harm you, plans to give you hope and a future."**
God has made a <u>DECLARATION</u> about the plans He has for me. He has not just said that He has plans; He has proclaimed it.

"For I know the plans I have for you," declares *the Lord,* **"plans to prosper you and not to harm you, plans to give you hope and a future."**
The <u>LORD</u> has made a declaration that He has plans for my life.

"For I know the plans I have for you," declares the Lord, "plans to *prosper* **you and not to harm you, plans to give you hope and a future."**
God has made plans to make me <u>PROSPEROUS</u>, which means that He intends for me to thrive and/or to be very successful in my calling.

"For I know the plans I have for you," declares the Lord, "plans to prosper you *and* **not to harm you, plans to give you hope** *and* **a future."**
God doesn't just want me to prosper. He also wants to give me hope and a future, both now and for eternity.

"For I know the plans I have for you," declares the Lord, "plans to prosper you and *not* **to harm you, plans to give you hope and a future."**
God wants to make it clear that, despite the hardships or troubles that might come my way, He does <u>NOT</u> want to harm me and never wants me to perceive it as punishment.

"For I know the plans I have for you," declares the Lord, "plans to prosper you and not *to harm* **you, plans to give you hope and a future."**
God's plans do not include anything that would cause <u>HARM</u>, injury, damage, or hurt to me.

"For I know the plans I have for you," declares the Lord, "plans to prosper you and not to harm you, plans to *give* **you hope and a future."**
God not only has the plans in His hands, He plans to <u>GIVE</u> the plans to me because in order for His plans to unfold, I must be in possession of them.

"For I know the plans I have for you," declares the Lord, "plans to prosper you and not to harm you, plans to give you *hope* **and a future."**
God wants me to have <u>HOPE</u>, or confident expectations, about the plans He has planned for me.

"For I know the plans I have for you," declares the Lord, "plans to prosper you and not to harm you, plans to give you hope and a *future.***"**
God has plans for me not only for today or tomorrow, but plans for my entire future both on this Earth and when I am living in His kingdom.

Chapter Two: The Seed Within Answer Key

Scripture Study: Planted in the Word

How Seed is Planted

* Seeds are planted by <u>God</u>.

  What is God referred to in John 15:1? Why do you think He is described this way?

  <u>God is referred to a gardener because He cultivates us to be fruitful.</u>

  There are many reasons why God might plant a seed. What are the reasons cited in Isaiah 60:21 and Isaiah 61:11?

  <u>God plants a seed to display His splendor and to make righteousness and praise spring up before all nations.</u>

  Read Matthew 6:26, which offers proof that we do not need to sow our own seed for nourishment, but can rely on God to feed us. What specific proof does this verse offer?

  <u>The birds do not sow or reap, and God feeds them, so He will do the same for us because we are even more valuable to him.</u>

  Like most Psalms, Psalm 92:12–14 was based upon historical events in the Old Testament (specifically about Abraham and Sarah), but also makes a statement in general for all believers of all times. What promise do these verses offer to the righteous who are planted in the house of the Lord?

  <u>These verses promise that those planted in the house of the Lord will flourish in the courts of God. They will still bear fruit in old age, and they will stay fresh and green, proclaiming that "the Lord is upright and He is my rock."</u>

  Who did God use to help with the seed planted in 1 Corinthians 3:6? <u>Paul and Apollos</u>

* Seeds can be and are planted by Satan, either directly or through society.

According to Isaiah 5:1–2, what was the resulting harvest of the one who planted the vineyard? <u>It yielded only bad fruit.</u>

As previously mentioned, God discusses the fall of Israel, using personification to help the readers of ancient times to understand the message. These concepts can be understood not only for Israel's past, but also by us today. According to Amos 5:11, why would the owner of the vineyard not drink its wine? <u>Because he trampled the poor and forced them to give him his grain.</u>

What message does this offer us today? <u>If we do not behave with moral and social integrity, we will not experience a spiritually fruitful life.</u>

Read the following verses and write down what you sow and reap, according to scripture.

Hosea 10:12: If you sow <u>righteousness</u>, you will reap <u>the fruit of unfailing love.</u>

Hosea 10:13: If you sow <u>wickedness</u>, you will reap <u>evil.</u>

Job 4:8: If you sow <u>trouble</u>, you will reap <u>trouble.</u>

Psalm 126:5: If you sow <u>tears</u>, you will reap <u>songs of joy.</u>

Proverbs 11:18: If you sow <u>righteousness</u>, you will reap <u>a sure reward.</u>

Proverbs 22:8: If you sow <u>wickedness</u>, you will reap <u>trouble.</u>

2 Corinthians 9:6: If you sow <u>sparingly</u>, you will reap <u>sparingly.</u> If you sow <u>generously</u>, you will reap <u>generously.</u>

Galatians 6:8: If you sow <u>to please your sinful nature</u>, you will reap <u>destruction.</u> If you sow <u>to please the Spirit</u>, you will reap <u>eternal life.</u>

James 3:8: If you sow <u>peace</u>, you will reap <u>a harvest of righteousness.</u>

<u>Effective Growth of Seed</u>

- Seeds need to be sown in fertile soil.

Read Luke 8:4–15 and answer the following questions.

What happened to the seed that was thrown on the path? <u>It was trampled on, and the birds of the air ate it up.</u>

What meaning did Jesus explain for this part of the parable? <u>The seed is the word of God. Those along the path are the ones who hear, and then the devil comes and takes away the word from their hearts, so that they may not believe and be saved.</u>

What happened to the seed that was scattered on the rock? <u>When it came up, the plants withered because they had no moisture.</u>

What meaning did Jesus explain for this part of the parable? <u>Those on the rock are the ones who receive the Word with joy when they hear it, but they have no root. They believe for a while, but after a time of testing they fall away.</u>

What happened to the seed that was sown among the thorns? <u>The thorns grew up with it and choked that plant.</u>

What meaning did Jesus explain for this part of the parable? <u>The seed that fell among thorns stands for those who hear, but as they go on their way, they are choked by life's worries, riches, and pleasures, and they do not mature.</u>

What happened to the seed that was sown among good soil? <u>It came up and yielded a crop that was a hundred times more than was sown.</u>

What meaning did Jesus explain for this part of the parable? <u>The seed on good soil stands for those with noble and good hearts, who hear the word, retain it, and produce a crop by persevering.</u>

- Seeds need the right conditions to sprout.

Ecclesiastes 11:6 instructs us to sow our seed in the morning, and at evening to not let our hands be idle, for we do not know which will succeed, whether this or that, or whether both will do equally well. What point do you think Solomon was trying to make when he wrote this verse? <u>If we sow our seed in the morning, it can be an active growth process throughout our day. Remember what happens when you sow positive seeds and know that if you sow goodness each morning, you will reap goodness throughout the day. But our responsibility to our harvest doesn't stop there; we must always "be about the business of our father" and should have no idle time where we aren't doing things that are pleasing to Him. Both will do well to assure that our harvest is abundantly overflowing.</u>

From the previous chapter, what soil conditions can you identify that are necessary for optimal growth of the good seed? <u>Faith, hope, and trust</u>

When God plants a seed, is the seed always destined to bear lots of fruit? Read the following verses to find out then write down a few modern reasons why a seed planted by God might not bear fruit today.

<u>Jeremiah 2:21</u>: I had planted you like a choice vine of sound and reliable stock. How then did you turn against me into a corrupt, wild vine?

<u>Jeremiah 11:17</u>: The LORD Almighty, who planted you, has decreed disaster for you, because the house of Israel and the house of Judah have done evil and provoked me to anger by burning incense to Baal.

Jeremiah 45:4: The LORD said, "Say this to him: 'This is what the LORD says: I will overthrow what I have built and uproot what I have planted, throughout the land.

James 1:21: Therefore, get rid of all moral filth and the evil that is so prevalent and humbly accept the word planted in you, which can save you.

Corruption and sin are present.
The person whom in the seed is planted has a love for other gods, such as money.
A Christian openly professes to follow Christ, but does not practice this in his/her home.
God is displeased by disobedience.
Moral filth is present, either actually or virtually.

- Seeds need strong root systems to become anchored and thrive.

Now look at the following picture.

What do you note about the roots, as compared to the plant? The roots remain consistent throughout the life of the plant, just as our God remains a consistent anchor for us.

Reread Luke 8:13. What does this verse say is responsible for roots not forming, which would mean there is no anchor present? The person believes for a while, but after a time of testing, falls away.

ℛelatable ℬible ℱigure

Abraham

According to Galatians 3:6–7, those who believe God just as Abraham believed are considered what? Children of Abraham.

As children of Abraham, what does Galatians 3:9 say we will receive because of our faith? Blessings just like those Abraham received.

According to Galatians 3:14, how do we receive the blessings given to Abraham? What blessings will we receive by faith? We will receive the blessings given to Abraham through Jesus Christ. By faith we will receive the promise of the Spirit.

Who does Paul clarify the seed represents in God's promise to Abraham in Galatians 3:16? Christ.

According to Galatians 3:21, who is an offspring of Abraham's seed? Anyone who belongs to Christ.

How does Galatians 3:21 describe those who are of Abraham's seed? As promised heirs to the Kingdom of God.

As we conclude this study of the scripture, read I Corinthians 15:35–44 and the ultimate promise that it holds for believers in Christ. What is this ultimate promise? There is a great promise in the life we will have after death. The body that is sown is perishable, but it is raised imperishable; it is sown in dishonor but raised in glory; it is sown in weakness and raised in power; it is sown as a natural body and raised as a spiritual body.

Chapter Three: Living Water Answer Key

Scripture Study: Saturated in the Word

Water from Above

Our foundation scripture this week talks about waiting for the season when God will shower you with blessings. What does Hosea 10:12 say we should do while we wait? We should seek the Lord (until He comes and showers righteousness on us).

How many showers does Joel 2:23 say God will send in His seasons? God will send abundant showers in both autumn and spring.

Read Isaiah 45:8. What does God command to happen? God commanded the heavens to rain down righteousness for salvation to spring up and righteousness to grow.

What does this mean in regard to your own personal situation? (Subjective answer)

Zechariah 10:1 is a wonderful passage of hope. To whom does the scripture say God gives plants of the field after He gives showers of rain? He gives plants of the field to everyone.

What do Genesis 24:35, Numbers 24:7, Job 36:26–28, Psalm 65:9–11, Psalm 68:9, Psalm 78:20, Joshua 17:14, and 1 Timothy 1:14 have in common? They all use the word abundantly to describe God how much water (or equivalent) God provides for us.

Effects of Water

- Water fills

  Read Psalm 65:9 below and circle all the verbs used in this passage.

  You care for the land and water it;
  you enrich it abundantly.
  The streams of God are filled with water
  to provide the people with grain,
  for so you have ordained it.

Read the following scriptures and identify what you can receive from the hand of God, as others have received it.

Exodus 31:2–4: <u>the Spirit of God</u>

Exodus 40:34 and Numbers 14:20–22: <u>the glory of the Lord</u>

Deuteronomy 34:8–10 and Luke 2:40: <u>the spirit of wisdom</u>

Job 8:21 and Psalm 126:2: <u>laughter</u>

Psalm 4:7: <u>heart with great joy</u>

Psalm 16:11, Psalm 126:3, Acts 2:28, and Acts 14:17: <u>joy</u>

Psalm 65:54 and Psalm 107:9: <u>good things</u>

Psalm 71:8: <u>praise</u>

Psalm 72:19: <u>glory</u>

Psalm 119:64: <u>love</u>

Isaiah 33:5: <u>justice and righteousness</u>

Habakkuk 2:14: <u>knowledge of the glory of the Lord</u>

Matthew 5:6: <u>righteousness</u>

Luke 1:15, Acts 13:52, Luke 1:41, and Luke 1:67: <u>Holy Spirit</u>

Romans 15:13: <u>joy and peace</u>

Ephesians 3:19: <u>fullness of God</u>

Philippians 1:11: <u>fruit of righteousness</u>

Colossians 1:9: <u>knowledge of his will</u>

1 Peter 1:8: <u>inexpressible and glorious joy</u>

What does Ephesians 1:22–23 say Christ fills and how? <u>It says He fills everything in every way.</u>

What does Ephesians 3:19–20 say will happen when you allow God's love to form roots in your life and know this love that surpasses knowledge? <u>You will be filled to the measure with all the fullness of God.</u>

- Water quenches

What confirmation does Isaiah 41:17–18 offer? What reassurance does verse 8 offer you?

This verse confirms that God will help the poor and needy as they search for water and find none, specifically noting that He will not forsake them. It should reassure those with infertility that, just as He made rivers flow on barren heights in this verse, He will provide the barren couple with water to quench their thirst for a child.

What other assurances does the Bible provide? Read the following scriptures and note the details of these blessed assurances.

Isaiah 55:1: God says, "Come all who are thirsty—water is free."

John 4:14: Whoever drinks the water Christ gives will never thirst. Indeed, the water he gives will become in them a spring of water welling up to eternal life.

John 6:35: Anyone who believes in Jesus will never be thirsty.

John 7:37–38: Streams of living water will flow from anyone who believes.

Revelation 21:6: In the end, God will still give water at no cost from the spring of the Water of Life.

- Water cleanses

Read Titus 3:3–8, which describes mankind being full of sin. How does this verse say we are saved from this sin? We are saved through the washing of rebirth and renewal by the Holy Spirit, whom He poured out on us generously through Jesus Christ our Savior.

What act is symbolic of our cleansing rebirth? The believer's baptism.

According to Psalm 51:7, how clean can God make you? God can make you as white as snow.

What do the following scriptures say that God cleans from us?

Ezekiel 36:25: He cleanses us from all impurities and from all idols.

Hebrews 9:14 and Hebrews 10:22: He cleanses our guilty consciences from acts that lead to death.

Jeremiah 33:8: He cleanses us from all the sins we have committed against Him.

I Corinthians 6:9–11: He cleanses us from our sinful behaviors.

How do Ezekiel 36:25 and Hebrews 10:22 say God washes us? He sprinkles us with clean/pure water.

- Water refreshes

  Whom do Psalm 68:9 and Jeremiah 31:25 say God refreshes? <u>God refreshes the weary.</u>

  What do Genesis 27:29, Hosea 14:5–6, Zechariah 8:12, and Deuteronomy 33:13 have in common? <u>They all discuss the blessings of heaven's dew, which God provides to us to help us grow.</u>

  How else does Acts 3:19 say we can receive refreshment from the Lord? <u>If we repent and turn to God so that our sins may be wiped out, we will receive times of refreshment from the Lord.</u>

  What should we do as a profession of our repentance from our previous life and acceptance of Christ as our Lord and Savior in our new spiritual life, according to Acts 2:38? Why should we do this? <u>We should be baptized in the name of Jesus Christ so our past sins will be forgiven, and we will receive the gift of the Holy Spirit.</u>

<u>Alterations in Water that Affect Growth</u>

- Drought

  Read the following scriptures and answer the questions below.

  This is what the LORD Almighty says: "Give careful thought to your ways. Go up into the mountains and bring down timber and build the house, so that I may take pleasure in it and be honored," says the LORD. "You expected much, but see, it turned out to be little. What you brought home, I blew away. Why?" declares the LORD Almighty. "Because of my house, which remains a ruin, while each of you is busy with his own house. Therefore, because of you the heavens have withheld their dew and the earth its crops. I called for a drought on the fields and the mountains, on the grain, the new wine, the oil and whatever the ground produces, on men and cattle, and on the labor of your hands." (Haggai 1:7-11)

  The LORD will turn the rain of your land into falling dust; it will descend on you from the sky until you are destroyed. (Deuteronomy 28:24)

  When the skies are shut and there is no rain, because they have sinned against You, and they pray toward this place and praise Your name, and they turn from their sins because You are afflicting them. (I Kings 8:35)

  Although he flourishes among [his] brothers, an east wind will come, a wind from the LORD rising up from the desert. His water source will fail, and his spring will run dry. The wind will plunder the treasury of every precious item. (Hosea 13:16)

  What do these verses have in common? <u>They all document proof that God caused droughts to happen in the Old Testament.</u>

  If I close the sky so there is no rain … and My people who are called by My name humble themselves, pray and seek My face, and turn from their evil ways, then I will hear from heaven, forgive their sin, and heal their land. My eyes will now be open and My ears attentive to prayer from this place. And I have now chosen and consecrated this temple so that My name may be there forever; My eyes and My heart will be there at all times. (2 Chronicles 7)

What does this verse say will cause God to heal those suffering a drought? <u>If they humble themselves, pray, seek God's face, and turn from their sinful ways.</u>

Read Isaiah 48:21. What does it say God did for those He led through the desert?

<u>He made water flow for them from the rock.</u>

Read Isaiah 44:3. What does God do when He pours water on the thirsty land and streams on the dry ground? <u>He will pour out his Spirit on your offspring and his blessing on your descendants.</u>

- Storms

  Did Jesus rescue the disciples from the storm because of their faith? <u>No, He rescued them in spite of their faith.</u>

  What was the disciples' response? <u>They were amazed by the supernatural way He saved them.</u>

Receiving the Living Water

Hosea 6:3 tells us that God will come to us like spring rain. What must we do to receive this rain? <u>We must acknowledge Him as our Lord.</u>

Who does John 4:13 specifically say gives Living Water? <u>Jesus.</u>

How does Acts Matthew 7:7–8 say that we get the Living Water from Jesus? <u>Ask and it will be given to you; seek and you will find; knock and the door will be opened to you. For everyone who asks receives; he who seeks finds; and to him who knocks, the door will be opened.</u>

How does Matthew 7:9–11 describe our relationship to God and his giving? <u>This compares us to a child asking for bread, noting that a father would not give him a stone. It points out that we are like the child to our Heavenly Father, and He will give us many good gifts to those who ask.</u>

What does James 4:3 say is a primary reason for unanswered prayers? <u>James 4:3 tells us that when we ask and do not receive, it's because we ask with wrong motives, that we may spend what we get on our pleasures.</u>

Ephesians 6:18: <u>Pray in the Spirit on all occasions with all kinds of prayers and requests.</u>

Colossians 4:2: <u>Devote yourselves to prayer, being watchful and thankful.</u>

Mark 11:24: <u>Whatever you ask for in prayer, believe that you have received it, and it will be yours.</u>

James 1:5–8: <u>If any of you lacks wisdom, he should ask God, who gives generously to all without finding fault, and it will be given to him. But when he asks, he must believe and not doubt, because he who doubts is like a wave of the sea, blown and tossed by the wind. That man should not think he will receive anything from the Lord; he is a double-minded man, unstable in all he does.</u>

Romans 12:12: <u>Be joyful in hope, patient in affliction, faithful in prayer.</u>

James 5:16–18: <u>Therefore confess your sins to each other and pray for each other so that you may be healed. The prayer of a righteous man is powerful and effective.</u>

Matthew 6:5–8: <u>Do not be like the hypocrites, for they love to pray standing in the synagogues and on the street corners to be seen by men. But when you pray, go into your room, close the door and pray to your Father, who is unseen. Then your Father, who sees what is done in secret, will reward you. And when you pray, do not keep on babbling like pagans, for they think they will be heard because of their many words. Do not be like them, for your Father knows what you need before you ask him.</u>

1 Thessalonians 5:16–18: <u>Be joyful always; pray continually; give thanks in all.</u>

Finally we come to the end of our prayer and say "in Jesus' name, Amen." Why did Jesus command us to pray in His name?

John 14:13–14: <u>Because Jesus said, "I will do whatever you ask in my name, so that the Son may bring glory to the Father. You may ask me for anything in my name, and I will do it."</u>

John 15:16: <u>Jesus said, "You did not choose me, but I chose you and appointed you to go and bear fruit—fruit that will last. Then the Father will give you whatever you ask in my name."</u>

John 16:24: <u>Jesus said "Until now you have not asked for anything in my name. Ask and you will receive, and your joy will be complete."</u>

Colossians 3:17: <u>We are instructed that whatever we do, whether in word or deed, we should do it all in the name of the Lord Jesus, giving thanks to God the Father through him.</u>

John 14:6: <u>Jesus said, "I am the way and the truth and the life. No one comes to the Father except through me."</u>

Does John 16:26 say that we pray in Jesus' name so that He will ask the Father on our behalf? <u>*No.* John clarifies that this is not the reason, but notes that we will receive favor from God because we have loved Jesus and have believed that He came from God.</u>

Relatable Bible Figure

The Woman at the Well

Read John 4:1–26. Where did Jesus say the Living Water comes from and what did He say it would do? <u>Jesus said the living water comes from Him and that those who drink of the living water will never thirst, but instead, the water He gives will become a spring of water welling up to eternal life.</u>

How did the woman at the well know it was really Jesus speaking to her? <u>He knew things about her that no other stranger could have known and He told her things that could only come from the promised Messiah.</u>

Reflection

The scriptures in today's study are just as real and applicable today as they were when first written. Take a minute to reflect on how a few of these scriptures can be applied directly to you and rewrite them as if they were originally meant only for you. The first one is done for you as an example.

- **You care for the land and water it; You enrich it abundantly. The streams of God are filled with water to provide the people with grain, for so you have ordained it. You drench its furrows and level its ridges; you soften it with showers and bless its crops. You crown the year with your bounty, and your carts overflow with abundance. (Psalm 65:9–11)**

   <u>You care for me and water me; You enrich me abundantly. The streams of God are filled with water to provide me with all I need, for so you have ordained it. You drench my furrows and level my ridges; You soften me with showers and bless me. You crown the year with your bounty, and your carts overflow with abundance.</u>

   They will neither hunger nor thirst, nor will the desert heat or sun beat upon them. He who has compassion on them will guide them and lead them beside springs of water. (Isaiah 49:10)

   <u>I will neither hunger nor thirst, nor will the desert heat or sun beat upon me. He who has compassion on then will guide me and lead me beside springs of water.</u>

   The Lord will guide you always; he will satisfy your needs in a sun-scorched land and will strengthen your frame. You will be like a well-watered garden, like a spring whose waters never fail. (Isaiah 58:11)

   <u>The Lord with guide me always; He will satisfy my needs in a sun-scorched land and will strengthen my frame. I will be like a well-watered garden, like a spring whose waters never fail.</u>

But his delight is in the law of the Lord, and on his law he meditates day and night. He is like a tree planted by streams of water, which yields its fruit in season and whose leaf does not wither. Whatever he does prospers. (Psalm 1:2–4)

But my delight is in the law of the Lord, and on his law I meditate day and night. I am like a tree planted by streams of water, which yields its fruit in season and whose leaf does not wither. Whatever I do prospers.

How priceless is your unfailing love! Both high and low among men find refuge in the shadow of your wings. They feast on the abundance of your house; you give them drink from your river of delights. For with you is the fountain of life; in your light we see light. - Psalm 36:7–9

How priceless is your unfailing love! I find refuge in the shadow of your wings. I feast on the abundance of your house; you give me drink from your river of delights. For with you is the fountain of life; in your light I see light.

Chapter Four: Abundant Light Answer Key

Scripture Study: Illuminating the Word

Our foundation scripture for this chapter notes that God will be the light for our path and will make the rough spots smooth. To which scripture from the previous study is this passage similar?

Psalm 65: 9–11, which states God will level the ridges.

What assurance does that give you? That God will be right beside me through the rough spots to make the difficult journey easy to bear.

- Light illuminates / makes visible

  You, O Lord, keep my lamp burning; my God turns my darkness into light. (Psalm 18:28)

  Send forth your light and your truth, let them guide me; let them bring me to your holy mountain, to the place where you dwell. (Psalm 43:3)

  For you have delivered me from death and my feet from stumbling, that I may walk before God in the light of life. (Psalm 56:13)

  Blessed are those who have learned to acclaim, who walk in the light of your presence. (Psalm 89:15)

  Light is shed upon the righteous and joy on the upright in heart. (Psalm 97:11)

  Your word is a lamp to my feet and a light for my path. (Psalm 119:105)

The above scriptures clearly define the role of God as a lamp providing light for the pathway. Summarize what these scriptures collectively say in one or two sentences. Remember to include to whom God provides light, how it is accomplished, and the outcome.

Summary: The Lord provides light to the path of the righteous and those who have learned to acclaim Him to keep their feet from stumbling and to guide them with the truth.

- Light clarifies

Read Psalm 13. Why was David asking God to give light to his eyes? <u>He wanted God to answer his question about why God hadn't conquered his enemy yet.</u>

David concludes Psalm 13 with confirmation of his faith in God. What does he say and why is this significant? <u>David says that he trusts in God's unfailing love, and his heart rejoices in God's salvation, noting that he will sing to the Lord because He has been good to him. It's significant because, despite David's bleak outlook, he recognized that God had been good to him in the past, and he knew that God would again be faithful. The importance is that he knew God.</u>

What does Ephesians 1:19 say should be enlightened and why? <u>It says the eyes of your heart should be enlightened so that you may know the hope to which He has called you, the riches of his glorious inheritance in the saints, and His incomparably great power for us who believe.</u>

- Light exposes

What does 1 Corinthians 4:5 say God will bring to light and expose? <u>It says He will bring to light what is hidden in darkness and will expose the motives of men's hearts.</u>

From the same scripture, what is the result of the exposure? <u>Each person will receive his praise from God.</u>

According to Psalm 90:8, can we hide any of our secret sins from God? <u>No, our secret sins are set before Him in the light of His presence.</u>

- Light brightens

Read Psalm 4:6–8. What does the Psalmist imply as the outcome of the Light of the Lord's face shining upon him? <u>He filled his heart with great joy and acknowledged that even in darkness, the light will dawn for him.</u>

According to Psalm 19:8, what provides light to our eyes? <u>The radiant commands of the Lord provide it.</u>

Read Psalm 112. What does the Psalmist say will happen for the gracious, compassionate, and righteous man who fears the Lord and finds great delight in His command? <u>Even in darkness the light will dawn for him.</u>

What other promises does Psalm 112 offer? Be specific with regard to your journey through infertility.

<u>Psalm 112 promises that I will have children, for my children will be mighty and my generation blessed.</u>

<u>My house will be full of wealth and riches.</u>

I will never be shaken, even though I may have a failed pregnancy or adoption attempt.

I will be remembered forever.

I will have no fear of bad news.

My heart will be steadfast, trusting in the Lord.

My heart will be secure with no fear.

I will look in triumph on my foes.

- Light provides protection

The following scriptures clearly define the role of God as a light-providing protector. Summarize what these scriptures collectively say by filling in the blank spaces in the two sentences below.

The Lord is my light and my salvation—whom shall I fear? The Lord is the stronghold of my life—of whom shall I be afraid? (Psalm 27:1)

It was not by their sword that they won the land, nor did their arm bring victory; it was your right hand, your arm, and the light of your face, for you loved them. (Psalm 44:3)

Even in darkness light dawns for the upright for the gracious and compassionate and righteous man. (Psalm 112:4)

Even the darkness will not be dark to you; the light will shine like the day for the darkness is as light to you. (Psalm 139:12)

Because the Lord is my light, my salvation, and the stronghold of my life, the darkness will not be dark for me, and I shall fear no one. If I am upright, gracious, compassionate, and righteous, the light will dawn for me in darkness, and I will have victory because of God's right hand, His arm, and the light of His face because he loves me.

For what reason does the Psalmist attribute God's continual light in our darkness in Psalm 139:12–13? Because we are his created beings, and He wants light for us. He created our inmost beings and knit us together in our mother's wombs.

Receiving God's Light

According to Psalms 119:130, what gives light? The unfolding of God's Word gives light.

What do you think David was implying when he used the word *unfolding*?

The Bible is written in layers of understanding, and we cannot get to another layer without uncovering the outer layers. We will be exposed to the simple concepts first and then to deeper, complex concepts later as our understanding grows.

Read the following scriptures and then write down the holy characteristic(s) associated with each one.

"Wealth and honor come from you; you are the ruler of all things. In your hands are strength and power to exalt and give strength to all." (1 Chronicles 29:12)

☑ Omnipotence   ☐ Omnipresence   ☐ Omniscience   ☐ Omnibenevolence

"To God belong wisdom and power; counsel and understanding are his." (Job 12:13)

☑ Omnipotence   ☐ Omnipresence   ☑ Omniscience   ☐ Omnibenevolence

"The Spirit of the LORD *will rest on him—the Spirit of wisdom and of understanding, the Spirit of counsel and of power, the Spirit of knowledge and of the fear of the* LORD.*" (Isaiah 11:2)*

☐ Omnipotence   ☐ Omnipresence   ☑ Omniscience   ☐ Omnibenevolence

"But Jesus beheld them, and said unto them, With men this is impossible; but with God all things are possible." (Matthew 19:26)

☑ Omnipotence   ☐ Omnipresence   ☐ Omniscience   ☐ Omnibenevolence

"O LORD *God Almighty, who is like you? You are mighty, O* LORD, *and your faithfulness surrounds you." (Psalm 89:8)*

☑ Omnipotence   ☐ Omnipresence   ☐ Omniscience   ☐ Omnibenevolence

"When Abram was ninety-nine years old, the LORD *appeared to him and said, "I am God Almighty." (Genesis 17:1)*

☑ Omnipotence   ☐ Omnipresence   ☐ Omniscience   ☐ Omnibenevolence

"For with God nothing shall be impossible." (Luke 1:37)

☑ Omnipotence   ☐ Omnipresence   ☐ Omniscience   ☐ Omnibenevolence

"Give thanks to the God of heaven, for His steadfast love endures forever." (Psalm 136:26)

☐ Omnipotence   ☐ Omnipresence   ☐ Omniscience   ☑ Omnibenevolence

"Great is our Lord and mighty in power; his understanding has no limit." (Psalm 147:5)

☑ Omnipotence   ☐ Omnipresence   ☑ Omniscience   ☐ Omnibenevolence

"Am I only a God nearby," declares the LORD, *"and not a God far away? Can anyone hide in secret places so that I cannot see him?" declares the* LORD. *"Do not I fill heaven and earth?" declares the* LORD. *(Jeremiah 23:23–24)*

☐ Omnipotence   ☑ Omnipresence   ☐ Omniscience   ☐ Omnibenevolence

"You are the God who performs miracles; you display your power among the peoples." (Psalm 77:14)

☑ Omnipotence   ☐ Omnipresence   ☐ Omniscience   ☐ Omnibenevolence

"They will tell of the power of your awesome works, and I will proclaim your great deeds." (Psalm 145:6)

☑ Omnipotence   ☐ Omnipresence   ☐ Omniscience   ☐ Omnibenevolence

"Lift your eyes and look to the heavens: Who created all these? He who brings out the starry host one by one, and calls them each by name. Because of his great power and mighty strength, not one of them is missing." (Isaiah 40:26)

☑ Omnipotence   ☐ Omnipresence   ☐ Omniscience   ☐ Omnibenevolence

"Ah, Sovereign LORD, you have made the heavens and the earth by your great power and outstretched arm. Nothing is too hard for you." (Jeremiah 32:17)

☑ Omnipotence   ☐ Omnipresence   ☐ Omniscience   ☐ Omnibenevolence

"By his power God raised the Lord from the dead, and He will raise us also." (1 Corinthians 6:14)

☑ Omnipotence   ☐ Omnipresence   ☐ Omniscience   ☐ Omnibenevolence

"For the kingdom of God is not a matter of talk but of power." (1 Corinthians 4:20)

☑ Omnipotence   ☐ Omnipresence   ☐ Omniscience   ☐ Omnibenevolence

"But we have this treasure in jars of clay to show that this all-surpassing power is from God and not from us." (2 Corinthians 4:7)

☑ Omnipotence   ☐ Omnipresence   ☐ Omniscience   ☐ Omnibenevolence

"I pray that out of his glorious riches He may strengthen you with power through his Spirit in your inner being, so that Christ may dwell in your hearts through faith." (Ephesians 3:16)

☑ Omnipotence   ☐ Omnipresence   ☐ Omniscience   ☐ Omnibenevolence

"I pray also that the eyes of your heart may be enlightened in order that you may know the hope to which He has called you, the riches of his glorious inheritance in the saints, and his incomparably great power for us who believe. That power is like the working of his mighty strength, which he exerted in Christ when he raised him from the dead and seated him at his right hand in the heavenly realms, far above all rule and authority, power and dominion, and every title that can be given, not only in the present age but also in the one to come." (Ephesians 1: 18–21)

☑ Omnipotence   ☐ Omnipresence   ☐ Omniscience   ☐ Omnibenevolence

"For God so loved the world, that he gave his only Son, that whoever believes in him should not perish but have eternal life." (John 3:16)

☐ Omnipotence   ☐ Omnipresence   ☐ Omniscience   ☑ Omnibenevolence

"And we pray this in order that you may live a life worthy of the Lord and may please him in every way: bearing fruit in every good work, growing in the knowledge of God, being strengthened with all power according to his glorious might so that you may have great endurance and patience, and joyfully giving thanks to the Father, who has qualified you to share in the inheritance of the saints in the kingdom of light." (Colossians 1:10–11)

☑ Omnipotence   ☐ Omnipresence   ☐ Omniscience   ☐ Omnibenevolence

"But God shows His love for us in that while we were still sinners, Christ died for us." (Romans 5:8)
☐ Omnipotence ☐ Omnipresence ☐ Omniscience ☑ Omnibenevolence

"But God, being rich in mercy, because of the great love with which He loved us, even when weere dead in our trespasses, made us alive together with Christ - by grace you have been saved..." (Ephesians 2:4-5)
☐ Omnipotence ☐ Omnipresence ☐ Omniscience ☑ Omnibenevolence

"His divine power has given us everything we need for life and godliness through our knowledge of him who called us by his own glory and goodness." (2 Peter 1:3)
☑ Omnipotence ☐ Omnipresence ☐ Omniscience ☐ Omnibenevolence

"By wisdom the Lord laid the earth's foundations, by understanding he set the heavens in place; by his knowledge the deeps were divided, and the clouds let drop the dew." (Proverbs 3:19–20)
☐ Omnipotence ☐ Omnipresence ☑ Omniscience ☐ Omnibenevolence

"How many are your works, O Lord! In wisdom you made them all." (Psalm 104:24)
☐ Omnipotence ☐ Omnipresence ☑ Omniscience ☐ Omnibenevolence

"Surely you desire truth in the inner parts; you teach me wisdom in the inmost place." (Psalm 51:6)
☐ Omnipotence ☐ Omnipresence ☑ Omniscience ☐ Omnibenevolence

"No, in all these things we are more than conquerors through Him who loved us. For I am sure that neither death nor life, nor angels nor rulers, nor things present nor things to come, nor powers, nor height nor depth, nor anything else in all creation, will be able to separate us from the love of God in Christ Jesus our Lord." (Romans 8:37-39)
☐ Omnipotence ☐ Omnipresence ☐ Omniscience ☑ Omnibenevolence

"For God, who said, "Let light shine out of darkness." made his light shine in our hearts to give us the light of the knowledge of the glory of God in the face of Christ." (2 Corinthians 4:6)
☐ Omnipotence ☐ Omnipresence ☑ Omniscience ☐ Omnibenevolence

"He will be the sure foundation for your times, a rich store of salvation and wisdom and knowledge." (Isaiah 33:6)
☐ Omnipotence ☐ Omnipresence ☑ Omniscience ☐ Omnibenevolence

"Then Daniel praised the God of heaven and said: "Praise be to the name of God forever and ever; wisdom and power are his." (Daniel 2:19–20)
☑ Omnipotence ☐ Omnipresence ☑ Omniscience ☐ Omnibenevolence

"He changes times and seasons; he sets up kings and deposes them. He gives wisdom to the wise and knowledge to the discerning." (Daniel 2:21)
☑ Omnipotence ☐ Omnipresence ☑ Omniscience ☐ Omnibenevolence

"Oh, the depth of the riches of the wisdom and knowledge of God! How unsearchable his judgments, and his paths beyond tracing out!" (Romans 11:33)

☐ Omnipotence ☐ Omnipresence ☑ Omniscience ☐ Omnibenevolence

In this the love of God was made manifest among us, that God sent His only Son into the world, so that we might live through Him. In this is love, not that we have loved God, but that He loved us and sent his Son to be the propitiation for our sins. Beloved, if God so loved us, we also ought to love one another." (1 John 2:4-5)

☐ Omnipotence ☐ Omnipresence ☐ Omniscience ☑ Omnibenevolence

"But the wisdom that comes from heaven is first of all pure; then peace-loving, considerate, submissive, full of mercy and good fruit, impartial and sincere." (James 3:17)

☐ Omnipotence ☐ Omnipresence ☑ Omniscience ☐ Omnibenevolence

"O Lord, you have searched me and you know me. You know when I sit and when I rise; you perceive my thoughts from afar. You discern my going out and my lying down; you are familiar with all my ways. Before a word is on my tongue you know it completely, O Lord." (Psalm 139: 1–4)

☐ Omnipotence ☑ Omnipresence ☑ Omniscience ☐ Omnibenevolence

"For this reason, since the day we heard about you, we have not stopped praying for you and asking God to fill you with the knowledge of his will through all spiritual wisdom and understanding." (Colossians 1:9)

☐ Omnipotence ☐ Omnipresence ☑ Omniscience ☐ Omnibenevolence

"My purpose is that they may be encouraged in heart and united in love, so that they may have the full riches of complete understanding, in order that they may know the mystery of God, namely, Christ, in whom are hidden all the treasures of wisdom and knowledge." (Colossians 2:2–3)

☐ Omnipotence ☐ Omnipresence ☑ Omniscience ☐ Omnibenevolence

Whoever does not love does not know God because God is love. (1 John 4:8)

☐ Omnipotence ☐ Omnipresence ☐ Omniscience ☑ Omnibenevolence

"Where can I go from your Spirit? Where can I flee from your presence? If I go up to the heavens, you are there; if I make my bed in the depths, you are there. If I rise on the wings of the dawn, if I settle on the far side of the sea, even there your hand will guide me, your right hand will hold me fast. If I say, "Surely the darkness will hide me and the light become night around me," even the darkness will not be dark to you; the night will shine like the day, for darkness is as light to you. For you created my inmost being; you knit me together in my mother's womb. I praise you because I am fearfully and wonderfully made; your works are wonderful, I know that full well. My frame was not hidden from you when I was made in the secret place. When I was woven together in the depths of the earth, your eyes saw my unformed body. All the days ordained for me were written in your book before one of them came to be. How precious to me are your thoughts,

O God! How vast is the sum of them! Were I to count them, they would outnumber the grains of sand. When I awake, I am still with you." (Psalm 139: 8–18)

☐ Omnipotence   ☑ Omnipresence   ☐ Omniscience   ☐ Omnibenevolence

"Finally, be strong in the Lord and in his mighty power." (Ephesians 6:10)

☑ Omnipotence   ☐ Omnipresence   ☐ Omniscience   ☐ Omnibenevolence

According to James 3:17, how is God's wisdom described? <u>God's wisdom is described as first of all pure; then peace-loving, considerate, submissive, full of mercy and good fruit, impartial and sincere.</u>

Why do you think it is described this way? <u>It is described as pure because everything that comes from God must be pure. It is peace-loving, considerate (of our specific needs), full of mercy and good fruit because these are the blessings that God provides us through his wisdom. It is impartial because God gives wisdom to anyone who seeks it. Finally, it is sincere because God doesn't provide anything that doesn't align with his will.</u>

How should you obtain wisdom that will light your path, according to James 1:5? <u>You should ask God, who gives generously to all without finding fault, and it will be given to you.</u>

Proverbs 2:6 confirms that wisdom is given by God. Where specifically does it say wisdom comes from? <u>From the mouth of the Lord.</u>

What else does Proverbs 2:7–9 say God will do for us? <u>He holds victory in store for the upright, He is a shield to those who walk blameless, for He guards the course of the just and protects the way of the faithful ones.</u>

According to Ecclesiastes 2:26, to whom does God give wisdom, knowledge, and happiness, and what does He give the sinner? <u>God gives wisdom, knowledge, and happiness to the man who pleases Him, but to the sinner He gives the task of gathering and storing up wealth to hand it over to the one who pleases God.</u>

What does 2 Peter 1:2 say we will receive in abundance through the knowledge of God and of Jesus? <u>Grace and peace.</u>

Being God's Light

What does Jesus call us in Matthew 5:13? <u>The Light of the World.</u>

What does He command us to do? <u>He commands us to let our light shine before men.</u>

Why is this important to God? <u>So others will see our good deeds and praise God.</u>

How does Matthew 6:22 say your light can be visible? <u>Matthew says your light can be visible through your eyes, noting that if your eyes are bad, your whole body will be full of great darkness.</u>

According to 2 Corinthians 4–6, God made his light shine in our hearts to give us the light of the knowledge of the glory of the God in the face of Christ. Why does the verse say some are blinded to this light? It says the god of this age has blinded the minds of unbelievers, so that they cannot see the light of the gospel of the glory of Christ, who is the image of God.

What are some "gods" existing today and doing the same thing? Money, lust, selfish pleasure, selfish ambition, and similar motivations.

Who, according to 2 Corinthians 11:14, masquerades as an angel of light while hoping to distract humans from God's light? Satan.

Relatable Bible Figure

Solomon

According to 2 Samuel 2:24, how did God feel about Solomon at the time of his birth? The Bible says the Lord loved him.

How does 2 Chronicles 1:1–10 say that Solomon obtained his great wisdom? Solomon specifically asked God for it.

In 2 Chronicles 1: 11–12, how did God reply to Solomon's request?

God said to Solomon, "Since this is your heart's desire and you have not asked for wealth, riches or honor, nor for the death of your enemies, and since you have not asked for a long life but for wisdom and knowledge to govern my people over whom I have made you king, therefore wisdom and knowledge will be given you. And I will also give you wealth, riches and honor, such as no king who was before you ever had and none after you will have."

Chapter Five: Destructive Forces Answer Key

Scripture Study: Defending with the Word

Types of Destructive Forces

- Weeds

According to 1 Timothy 6:10, what is another negative root? Why is it so bad? The love of money is a negative root because some people, eager for money, have wandered from the faith and pierced themselves with many griefs.

According to Matthew 15:13, what specifically will God pull up by the roots? Every plant that He has not planted will be pulled up by the roots.

What types of behaviors can have such devastating effects on your spiritual growth? Read the following scriptures and identify the weeds below.

Proverbs 28:25: greed and dissent

1 John 2:15: love of the things of the world

1 John 2:16: cravings, lust, and boasting

Titus 2:12: ungodliness and worldly passions

1 Corinthians 3:3: jealousy and quarreling

Galatians 5:26: conceit, provoking and envying each other

Philippians 2:3: selfish ambition and vain conceit

Galatians 5:19–21: sexual immorality, impurity and debauchery; idolatry and witchcraft; hatred, discord, jealousy, fits of rage, selfish ambition, dissent, factions, and envy; drunkenness, orgies

Romans 1:29–30: every kind of wickedness, evil, greed and depravity. They are full of envy, murder, strife, deceit and malice. gossip, slander, God-haters, insolence, arrogance, boastfulness

James 2:1: favoritism

Romans 13:2: rebellion against authority

Ephesians 6:4: exasperating children

Matthew 7:1: judging others

Proverbs 12:22: lying

- Where does Mark 7:21–23 say specific weeds come from? Mark says these evils come from inside, from within a man's heart.

  Who is responsible for the weeds, according to Matthew 13:38–39? The weeds are the sons of the evil one, and the enemy who sows them is the devil.

- Pests

  Instead, how does Matthew 18:15 say we should respond when a Christian sins against us? We should go to that person and show him his fault, just between the two of us.

  According to Matthew 18: 21–22, how many times should we forgive someone? Seventy-seven times, or essentially as often as he or she needs it.

  In 2 Timothy 3–7, Paul describes pests who are "lovers of themselves, lovers of money, boastful, proud, abusive, disobedient to their parents, ungrateful, unholy, without love, unforgiving, slanderous, without self-control, brutal, not lovers of the good, treacherous, rash, conceited, lovers of pleasure rather than lovers of God … the kind who worm their way into homes and gain control over weak-willed women, who are loaded down with sins and are swayed by all kinds of evil desires."

  What does Timothy instruct us to do with them? Have nothing to do with them.

  How does Matthew 7:15 describe them? As ones who come to in sheep's clothing, but inwardly are ferocious wolves.

  How does Matthew 7:16–20 say we will be able to know these people are weeds? We will know them by their fruit, noting that every good tree bears good fruit, but a bad tree bears bad fruit. A good tree cannot bear bad fruit, and a bad tree cannot bear good fruit. Thus, by their fruit you will recognize them.

  Read 2 Peter 2, which describes the path of the false teachers. What does this chapter say will happen to them because of what they do to us? God will punish them.

  How else does the Word say God has and will punish the wicked? Read the following scriptures and document the method.

Psalm 107: 33–34: He turned rivers into a desert, flowing springs into thirsty ground, and fruitful land into a salt waste.

Psalm 58:9: The wicked will be swept away quickly.

Psalm 11:6: He will rain fiery coals and burning sulfur on the wicked.

1 Samuel 2:8–10: The wicked will be silenced in darkness.

What does Deuteronomy 28:38 describe as the outcome of your life if you follow a sinful path? You will sow much seed in the field but you will harvest little, because locusts will devour it.

Read Proverbs 16:4–6. What three concepts do these verses reinforce from our current and previous study together? What do you think the author meant when He wrote "through the fear of the Lord a man avoids evil"? These verses reinforce that 1.) God works everything out consistently with His will for a particular person, 2.) God will punish those who choose to live a life of sin, and 3.) Because He is a loving and faithful God, he will forgive the sins of those who ask for cleansing. The fear refers to the fear that we, as believers should have towards the punishment that God can instill on our lives if we do not repent of our sins and live a life pleasing to Him.

Protection from Destructive Forces

- God as a weed barrier

  What specific promise does God offer to reinforce his role as weed barrier in Malachi 3:11? God said, "I will prevent pests from devouring your crops, and the vines in your fields will not cast their fruit."

  In Chapter Two we studied the parable of the seed that fell among the thorns, which grew up and choked the plants. Revisit Luke 8:14 to identify again the meaning of this part of the parable. Write your answer below. The seed that fell among thorns stands for those who hear, but as they go on their way, they are choked by life's worries, riches, and pleasures, and they do not mature.

  In contrast, how does Luke 8:15 say to ensure a bountiful crop? The seed should be planted in good soil, which means we should have noble and good hearts and hear the word, retain it, and persevere.

  What specific instruction does Romans 12:2 give us for us to retain? Do not conform any longer to the pattern of this world, but be transformed by the renewing of your mind so you will be able to test and approve what God's will is—his good, pleasing and perfect will.

  The book of Matthew offers insight into the contrast between following a path of sin and a path that leads to life spent in fertile soil. How is this path described in Matthew 7:13, and which way should you go? Matthew describes the road that leads to destruction as broad, with a wide gate, so many may enter through it. In contrast, he describes the life gate as being small and the road narrow. He instructs us to go through the narrow gate.

<u>But how do you know which is the narrow gate? I'm sure, after the last chapter, that you have a pretty good idea, but read Proverbs 4 and underline all the instructions contained within the Word.</u>

<u>Proverbs 4</u>

1 *Listen, my sons, to a father's instruction;*
  pay attention and gain understanding.

2 *I give you sound learning,*
  so do not forsake my teaching.

3 *When I was a boy in my father's house,*
  still tender, and an only child of my mother,

4 *he taught me and said,*
  "Lay hold of my words with all your heart;
  keep my commands and you will live.

5 *Get wisdom, get understanding;*
  do not forget my words or swerve from them.

6 *Do not forsake wisdom, and she will protect you;*
  love her, and she will watch over you.

7 *Wisdom is supreme; therefore get wisdom.*
  Though it cost all you have, get understanding.

8 *Esteem her, and she will exalt you;*
  embrace her, and she will honor you.

9 *She will set a garland of grace on your head*
  and present you with a crown of splendor."

10 *Listen, my son, accept what I say,*
   and the years of your life will be many.

11 *I guide you in the way of wisdom*
   and lead you along straight paths.

12 *When you walk, your steps will not be hampered;*
   when you run, you will not stumble.

13 *Hold on to instruction, do not let it go;*
   guard it well, for it is your life.

14 *Do not set foot on the path of the wicked*
   or walk in the way of evil men.

15 *Avoid it, do not travel on it;*
   turn from it and go on your way.

16 *For they cannot sleep till they do evil;*
   they are robbed of slumber till they make someone fall.

17 *They eat the bread of wickedness*
   and drink the wine of violence.

18 *The path of the righteous is like the first gleam of dawn,*
   shining ever brighter till the full light of day.

19 *But the way of the wicked is like deep darkness;*

they do not know what makes them stumble.
20 **My son, pay attention to what I say;**
listen closely to my words.
21 **Do not let them out of your sight,**
keep them within your heart;
22 **for they are life to those who find them**
and health to a man's whole body.
23 **Above all else, guard your heart,**
for it is the wellspring of life.
24 **Put away perversity from your mouth;**
keep corrupt talk far from your lips.
25 **Let your eyes look straight ahead,**
fix your gaze directly before you.
26 **Make level paths for your feet**
and take only ways that are firm.
27 **Do not swerve to the right or the left;**
keep your foot from evil.

The Bible offers many wise instructions on how to avoid evil ones snatching you from the path you walk with God, yet there are times when pests just seem to appear out of nowhere, trying to tempt you to leave the safe, bright path of the Lord. What does Psalm 37:7 say you should do when this happens? Be still before the Lord and wait patiently for him; do not fret when men succeed in their ways, when they carry out their wicked schemes.

Read the following scriptures that relate to God as a physical barrier.

Genesis 15:1	*2 Samuel 22:31*	*Psalm 3:3*	*Psalm 5:12*
Psalm 18:30	*Psalm 18:35*	*Psalm 28:7*	*Psalm 33:20*
Psalm 84:11	*Psalm 119:114*	*Proverbs 30:5*	

What do they have in common? They all refer to God as a shield.

What does this figurative usage mean to you? It means that no matter what outside influences try to attack my soil, I am protected because the Lord will keep them from invading me.

What does the author of Psalm 84 say of his preference for God as his shield, and why? He says he would rather spend one day in God's courts as a doorkeeper in the house of God than a thousand days in the tents of the wicked because God bestows favor and honor and withholds no good thing from those whose walk is blameless.

• Mulch

What does 1 Thessalonians 5:11 instruct us to do? It tells us to encourage one another and build each other up.

In Romans 1:11–12, what does Paul say we should use to help each other? <u>He says we should help each other with the faith we have.</u>

In addition to encouraging one another, what additional instructions does Hebrews 10:25 provide? <u>Let us not give up meeting together as some are in the habit of doing.</u>

According to Matthew 18:20, what is the benefit of coming together? <u>Where two or three come together in God's name, there He is with them.</u>

- Fertilizer

Who does 2 Corinthians 1:3 say provides comfort to us and how does it say that comfort is used? <u>God comforts us in all our troubles, so that we can comfort those in any trouble with the comfort we ourselves receive from God.</u>

- Repellant

What does 1 Peter 5:8 say the enemy does? <u>The enemy the devil prowls around like a roaring lion looking for someone to devour.</u>

What four things does 1 Peter 5:8 and 9 instruct us to do? <u>1. Be alert, 2. Be of sober mind, 3. Resist the Devil, and 4. Stand firm in the faith</u>

Read the following and underline all of the instructions this verse provides.

Ephesians 6:10–18: Finally, <u>be strong in the Lord and in his mighty power.</u> <u>Put on the full armor of God so that you can take your stand against the devil's schemes.</u> For our struggle is not against flesh and blood, but against the rulers, against the authorities, against the powers of this dark world and against the spiritual forces of evil in the heavenly realms. Therefore <u>put on the full armor of God, so that when the day of evil comes, you may be able to stand your ground, and after you have done everything, to stand.</u> <u>Stand firm then, with the belt of truth buckled around your waist, with the breastplate of righteousness in place, and with your feet fitted with the readiness that comes from the gospel of peace.</u> In addition to all this, <u>take up the shield of faith, with which you can extinguish all the flaming arrows of the evil one.</u> <u>Take the helmet of salvation and the sword of the Spirit, which is the word of God.</u> And <u>pray in the Spirit on all occasions with all kinds of prayers and requests.</u> With this in mind, <u>be alert and always keep on praying for all the saints.</u>

Relatable Bible Figures

Martha and Mary

What was Jesus' response to her as found in Luke 10:41–42? <u>"Martha, Martha," the Lord answered, "you are worried and upset about many things, but only one thing is needed. Mary has chosen what is better, and it will not be taken away from her."</u>

Chapter Six: Reaping the Harvest Answer Key

Scripture Study: Harvesting the Fruit of the Word

Putting it All Together

- What it takes to have a spiritual harvest

Read John 3:16, Acts 16:13, Romans 10:9, and John 20:31. What do they all have in common? <u>They all note that you simply have to believe in Christ to be saved and have everlasting life.</u>

What does John 15:1 say about how we are trimmed and pruned and why it is necessary? <u>It says that God cuts off the branches that bear no fruit, while every fruit that does bear fruit he prunes, so that it will be even more fruitful.</u>

Read Romans 11 to find the correct answer to the following questions.

Why did God break off the branches of the Israelites?

- ☑ The Israelites were disobedient, unbelieving, and rejected God
- ☐ The Israelites were so obedient that God wanted to transplant them to form other fruitful trees.
- ☐ The Israelites broke themselves off to show their faithfulness to Christ.
- ☐ God accidentally broke the Israelites branches.

Who did God graft into the space where the branches were broken off?

- ☐ remnants of obedient Israelites as a reward
- ☐ disobedient Israelites as a means of salvation
- ☐ Gentiles, as a means of reward
- ☑ Gentiles, because of their faith

How did Paul refer to the Gentiles in Romans 11:17?

- ☐ a fruitful olive tree
- ☐ a sturdy olive branch
- ☑ a wild olive shoot
- ☐ a flavorful olive

Why did God graft the Gentiles into Himself?

☐ so they could share in the nourishing sap from His root
☐ to make the Israelites jealous
☐ to show the Gentiles His mercy
☑ all of the above

What warning was given to the Gentiles?

☑ not to have boastfulness or arrogance because this might cause them to be broken off just like the Israelites
☐ not to associate with any Israelites because they might become corrupted
☐ not to spread the gospel because they might not fully understand what they are teaching
☐ not to eat holy bread because it might contain some unholy ingredients

Did Paul say the branches that were broken off could never part of God again?

☐ Yes—he said that the branches would be removed and then burned.
☐ No—he said that the branches could be grafted back in after six years.
☑ No—he said the branches could be grafted back in if the Israelites reconciled with him and believed.
☐ No—he said the branches would be automatically grafted back in after the Gentiles had successfully   taken root with God.

- Ensuring growth

What does God command the seed-bearing plants and trees on the land to bear?

☐ fruits with seeds in it, according to their various kinds
☐ fruit with seed in it, according to their singular kind
☑ fruit with seed in it, according to their various kinds
☐ fruits with seeds in it, according to their singular kind

According to John 15: 4, what else does Jesus say is necessary to bear fruit? Why? We must remain in Him and then He will remain in us because no branch can bear fruit by itself; it must remain on the vine. Neither can we bear fruit unless we remain in him.

What does John 15:6 say will happen to those who do not remain in him? They are like a branches that are thrown away and withered, and will be placed into the fire and burned, which implies that those people will not enter the heavenly kingdom, but will instead burn in hell.

In contrast, what promise is given to those who remain in Christ and allow His Words to remain in them, according to John 15:7? They may ask whatever they wish and it will be given to them, and they will bear much fruit because they have proven themselves to be disciples of Christ.

Therefore, since we are surrounded by such a great cloud of witnesses, let us throw off everything that hinders and the sin that so easily entangles, and let us run with <u>perseverance</u> the race marked out for us. (Hebrew 12:1)

You need to <u>persevere</u> so that when you have done the will of God, you will receive what he has promised. (Hebrews 10:36)

Blessed is the man who <u>perseveres</u> under trial, because when he has stood the test, he will receive the crown of life that God has promised to those who love him. (James 1:12)

As you know, we consider blessed those who have <u>persevered</u>. You have heard of Job's <u>perseverance</u> and have seen what the Lord finally brought about. The Lord is full of compassion and mercy. (James 5:11)

(Love) always protects, always trusts, always hopes, always <u>perseveres</u>. (1 Corinthians 13:7)

Therefore, since we have been justified through faith, we have peace with God through our Lord Jesus Christ, through whom we have gained access by faith into this grace in which we now stand. And we rejoice in the hope of the glory of God. Not only so, but we also rejoice in our sufferings, because we know that suffering produces <u>perseverance</u>; <u>perseverance</u>, character; and character, hope. And hope does not disappoint us, because God has poured out his love into our hearts by the Holy Spirit, whom he has given us. (Romans 5:1-5)

Consider it pure joy, my brothers, whenever you face trials of many kinds, because you know that the testing of your faith develops <u>perseverance</u>. <u>Perseverance</u> must finish its work so that you may be mature and complete, not lacking anything. (James 1:2-4)

How does Philippians 4:49 say you can keep your soil pure and ultimately acquire peace? *<u>Whatever is true, whatever is noble, whatever is right, whatever is pure, whatever is lovely, whatever is admirable—if anything is excellent or praiseworthy—think about such things. Whatever you have learned or received or heard from Christ, or seen Him—put it into practice. And the God of peace will be with you.</u>*

How do the following scriptures describe God's love, which is a component of holy seeds? Exodus 15:13, Psalm 6:4, Psalm 13:5, Psalm 21:7, Psalm 31:16, Psalm 32:10, Psalm 33:5, Psalm 33:18, Psalm 36:7, Psalm 44:26, Psalm 48:9, Psalm 51:1, Psalm 52:8, Psalm 85:7, Psalm 9:14, Psalm 107:8, 15, 21, and 31; Psalm 119:41, Psalm 119:76, Psalm 130:7, Psalm 143:8, Psalm 143:12, Psalm 147:11, Isaiah 54:10, Lamentations 3:32, and Hosea 10:12. <u>They all describe God's love as unfailing. By remembering this, you can place all your hope, faith, and trust in the promise that your efforts to grow God's seed will not fail.</u>

What does Deuteronomy 22:9 say you should remember when planting seeds? <u>Do not plant two kinds of seeds. If you do, not only with the crops you plant, but also the fruit will be defiled. This means that you can't plant both seeds for God and for man. All your seeds should be for and of God.</u>

How do you receive rain in its season for you to bear fruit for harvest, according to Leviticus 26:3? <u>You will receive rain if you follow God's decrees and are careful to obey his commands.</u>

What does Matthew 7 say we need to keep up with if we are to produce fruit? <u>We produce fruit in keeping with repentance.</u>

How do you achieve the fruit of the light, according to Ephesians 5:8–10? <u>You should live according to the light (for the fruit of the light consists in all goodness, righteousness, and truth) and find out what pleases the Lord.</u>

What does Ephesians 5:11 say you should do with fruitless deeds of the darkness<u>? Have nothing to do with them, but rather expose them.</u>

What do both Proverbs 18:20 and Hebrews 13:15 say about praising God? <u>From the fruit of his mouth is a man's stomach filled; with the harvest from his lips he is satisfied. Through Jesus, therefore, let us continually offer a sacrifice of praise—the fruit of the lips that confess His name. This confirms the role of praise in fruitfulness and the subsequent satisfaction that comes from it.</u>

How can we be assured that we can become fruitful according to John 15:16? <u>We can be assured because we did not choose God, but He chose us and appointed us to go and bear fruit that will last.</u>

<u>How to Recognize Fruitfulness</u>

• Fruit of the Spirit is abundantly visible

Review Galatians 5:22 and fill in the fruit of the Spirit below, based on what you will be receiving in exchange for a negative attribute or behavior.

hatred for <u>love</u>

sorrow for <u>joy</u>

anxiety for <u>peace</u>

impatience for <u>patience</u>

anger for <u>kindness</u>

wickedness for <u>goodness</u>

faithlessness for <u>faithfulness</u>

harshness for <u>gentleness</u>

unrestraint for <u>self-control</u>

- Blessings shower from above

Read the following scriptures and note the promise of blessings that are written.

Psalm 128: <u>It promises that I will eat the fruit of my labor and that blessings and prosperity will be mine. It also reminds me that I will be like a fruitful vine in my house, and my sons will be like olive shoots around my table, which also implies great blessings.</u>

1 Corinthians 9:23: <u>I do all this for the sake of the gospel, that I may share in its blessings. Do you not know that in a race all the runners run, but only one gets the prize? Run in such a way as to get the prize.</u>

Ephesians 1:3: <u>Praise be to the God and Father of our Lord Jesus Christ, who has blessed us in the heavenly realms with every spiritual blessing in Christ.</u>

<u>Enhancing the Fruitfulness of Others</u>

- Sharing your harvest

In Psalm 78:4, according to David, whom will we tell of the praiseworthy deeds of the Lord, his power, and the wonders he has done? <u>The next generation.</u>

What does Colossians tell us the gospel is doing all over the world? All over the world this gospel is bearing fruit and growing, just as it has been doing among you since the day the apostles first heard it and understood God's grace in all its truth.

- Cross-pollination

What does Romans 1:11–12 command us to do, and why? <u>Help each other with the faith we have because your faith will help me, and mine will help you.</u>

Relatable Bible Figure

<u>Jesus</u>

According to Leviticus 23, who established these feasts? *<u>God</u>*

Read the entire chapter of Leviticus 23 and fill in the name of the feast below.

Feast	Timing	Purpose	Prophetic Significance
The Feast of Passover	The fourteenth day of the first month at twillight	Passover was meant to commemorate Isreal's deliverance from Egypt, including the 'passover' by which Jews were spared the death of their firstborn through the blood of a lamb placed above their door.	This feast represents Jesus as our Passover, the Lamb of God who was sacrificed, and whose blood was received and applied so the wrath of God would pass us over. It speaks of redemption as a result of Jesus dying on the cross for our sins. This prophetic statement was complete when Jesus died on the cross on the exact day of the Feast of Passover.
The Feast of Unleavened Bread	The fifteenth day of each month for seven days	This feast showed the purity Israel was to walk in (illustrated by eating only bread without leaven, a type of sin) after the blood-deliverance of Passover.	This feast relates to the time of Jesus' burial during which he as received by God as holy and complete. It speaks of sanctification. Jesus was set apart. His body would not decay in the grave. This prophetic statement was complete when Jesus was placed in a tomb during the Feast of Unleavened Bread.
The Feast of Firstfruits	The day following the Passover's Sabbath	This feast was a time to give the firstfruits of harvest to God, including the first ripened stalks of grain in anticipation of a greater harvest to come.	The feast of the firstfruits relates to the resurrection of Jesus, who was the first human to receive resurrection. It speaks of the Lord's triumphant resurrection in which death simply could not hold her foe. This prophetic statement was complete on the third day when Jesus rose victoriously from the grave, which was, in fact, on the day of the Feast of the Firstfruits.

The Feast of Weeks or Pentecost	Fifty days after the seventh Sabbath.	This feast signified the completion of the wheat harvest and Israelites were to bring a new grain offering to the Lord.	This feast symbolizes Jesus giving us the gift of the Holy Spirit which inaugurated the New Covenant and Church Age. It speaks of origination signifying our origin as being from Christ when we are reborn. This prophetic statement was complete when the Holy Spirit was given on the exact day of the Feast of Weeks.
The Feast of Trumpets	The first day of the seventh month (which was also the first day of the first month of the Hebrew calendar).	This feast was a day of rest with a memorial blowing of trumpets to begin ten days of awe before the Day of Atonement in which the Israelites reflected on their sin and the need for atonement.	This feast symbolizes the rapture of the church that begins with the sound of a trumpet.
The Feast of Tabernacles	The fifteenth day of the seventh month	This feast was a time to rejoice in God's deliverance and provision for Israel during the time of wilderness wandering.	This feast is symbolic of the millennium, specifically the rest, peace, and comfort that God will bring us when He delivers us from this earth.